Tell Me the Story of Joseph

by Reed R. Simonsen

Thank yous!

Chad and Jim Fugate, Nelson Wadsworth, MaryAnne Pedersen, Brooke Martin, Claire Bloom, Paul Asay, Esq., Peter Simonsen, Jim Jepson, and my parents without whom I could not have accomplished this book or most anything else on this planet.

Copyright © MMV - MMXVII Reed R. Simonsen, all rights reserved.
The Joseph Smith Daguerreotype: Was the Prophet Photographed? by Reed Simonsen &
Chad Fugate. copyright 1993-2017 Reed Simonsen, all rights reserved.

Notice and rationale for Fair Use of Copyrighted material herein. Under the Fair Use
Clause of US Copyright Law.

Most of the illustrations and material used herein is used with permission or is part of
the public domain, however, there are a few items in which copyright claims are held by
various holders. US Copyright Law allows for Fair Use of other holders
copyrighted material under specific conditions. Our use under these
conditions can be found in the "Notes & Rationale for Fair Use section."

The author wishes to state that no part of this publication was authorized or reviewed in any way by any religious denomination or organization. The author alone is responsible for all content and opinions herein.

Please note: Due to the nature of varying book distribution channels currently available, eVersions of this book may contain different formats, explanations, illustrations and commentary from the printed version. This is beyond the control of the author.

A few grammatical corrections and typos have been corrected as brought to the authors attention from previous releases. Also various quotes and stories have been clarified for better expression in modern terms or have been simplified for children. Readers are encouraged to study out additional knowledge and desires from the best non-fictional accounts of the Church.

This is release Joseph (1.3c) and Daguerreotype (1.0)

Those readers wanting a more in-depth scholarly discussion of the life and teachings of Joseph Smith are encourage to study the Gospel Feast Series, Vol.1: *Daniel & the Last Days*; Vol. 2: *Jonah and the Great Plan of Happiness*; Vol. 3: *Ruth & the Saviours on Mount Zion*; and Vol. 4: *Zechariah & the Teachers of Righteousness* are now available.

Table of Contents

A December's Journey	v
1st - What is a Prophet?	1
2nd - Growing Up	5
3rd - One Last Commission	9
4th - A Golden Book from a Warrior Prophet	13
5th - The Book of Mormon	19
6th - Oliver Cowdery	27
7th - Witnesses to the Latter-day Work	33
8th - The Church of Jesus Christ of Latter-day Saints	37
9th - Safety in the Wilderness	43
10th - Zion City	47
11th - Power from On High	53
12th - Trouble in Zion	59
13th - Zion's Camp	63
14th - Glimpses of Kirtland	71
15th - The Central Place	77
16th - Brother Smith goes to Washington	81
17th - The City Beautiful	87
18th - A Prophet and a Brother	91
19th - A Man of God	97
20th - The King Follett Sermon	101
21st - Brother Joseph	107
22nd - A Prophet Martyred	113
23rd - None Greater But the Lord Himself	119
Bonus Chapter: The Joseph Smith Daguerreotype	123
Rationale for Fair Use & Endnotes	153

About the Author

Reed Simonsen grew up telling stories and entertaining people. He made his first short film at the age of eight. Convinced it would be a masterpiece, he spent his entire allowance on props and costumes. It was to climax with the most expensive scene of the film: "The Great Pie Fight." At a cost of $7 there could be only one take. The actors hit their marks without a hitch. Everything went perfectly until Reed discovered he had forgotten to put film in the camera! Over the next several years, lots of stuff happened.

Reed attended the University of Utah where he received a bachelor's in English. He worked for Paradigm Motion Picture Company writing budgets, film proposals, and coverage for film projects. He has made three documentaries; his favorite being an interview with Cecil B. DeMille's costume and production artist (in his 90's) from "The Ten Commandments."

He has written twelve books, including two best sellers.

He is actively involved in numerous charities from art preservation to childhood literacy. Reed's educational film proposal on child sex trafficking in Asia was presented to UNICEF, where it is still being considered. In 2004, Reed was honored for his charity work by Rotary International District 5420 with a Paul Harris Fellow. It was presented by the Vice President of Thailand, Mr. Bhichai Rattakul in a home town ceremony.

In 2006, a life long dream came true when Reed was accepted into the Directing Track, Master's Program at the School of Cinematic Arts at the University of Southern California. He has worked with, studied under, and has been mentored by many talented professionals, including; Joe B. Wallenstein, Tom Abrams, Kate Amend, Johanna Demetrakas, Helaine Head, Eric Furie, John Watson, Robert Zemeckis, and Steven Zuckerman. He has also learned how to effectively load film into a camera.

He is currently living in Studio City, California and is looking for a Mormon wife who can cope with his eccentric personality and who likes horses, dogs, all kinds of birds and certain cats.

Cover Art: *Joseph Smith in Nauvoo. 1840* by Theodore Gorka © Intellectual Reserve, Inc. Used with Permission.

Foreword
A December's Journey

Amid the frosty snow of rural Vermont, a new born baby's cry was all the world heard of the angel's rejoicing. The year was 1805 A.D. It was December the 23rd.

The Prophet Daniel had foretold the End of Days and millions of Jews and Christians worldwide saw the Great Hour of Judgment from Almighty God as eminent. Christianity knew that the Beloved Apostle John while on the Island of Patmos had said that before that terrible day, God would send one last commission to "seal" those who could be saved from the wrath of the coming Lamb.

But what did that mean?

Men and women in the New World had wrestled their political freedom from age old tyrants and in the Old World, *commoners* were toppling thrones. Even the fear of popes and priests had dwindled down to nothing!

Christianity had fractured into so many pieces that men began to speak of their God given right to worship according to the dictates of their own consciences. Some would claim that in reality there was no God at all.

What nearly no one on Earth could have guessed, although in retrospect it was there all the time, was this: God was about to do what He had always done. Call another prophet and speak His will again to the Earth.

It is the testimony of millions of living and departed Latter-day Saints, that Joseph Smith Jr., was the prophet called of God to prepare one last dispensation of Gospel purity so that the coming Day of Judgement would not be a day of total devastation. Those willing to embrace the final commission and be "sealed" to the Father as John had foretold would find themselves prepared and ready to greet the returning Jesus Christ on His terms. After all, you cannot put new wine into old bottles. That much the Lord God had already said.

The little book you hold was originally written as a gift of celebration to mark the anniversary of the 200th birthday of the Prophet Joseph Smith. Since Joseph was born only two days before Christmas, it occurred to me that it might be fun to celebrate his birth that year by gathering as a family and sharing one chapter a night (starting on December 1st) and ending on his birthday, December 23rd. This would leave Christmas Eve and Christmas Day for the *Gospel of Luke* and the Nativity of our Lord and Savior Jesus Christ; which is of course the sole purpose of the Holiday Season. My hope then is my hope now: that you will discover that to love Joseph Smith is to love Jesus Christ.

It has been over 10 years since that Christmas and it has been both humbling and joyful to me to have seen that little book reproduced thousands of times. I have met families from as far away as mother England who have told me that they so enjoyed the experience; that it has become one of their family's joyous Christmas traditions. Some of their children, now parents themselves, have passed it along. I have even heard kind words from church leaders whose names I don't have permission to print. One much beloved leader said, "Thank you! I love this little book. I love EVERY SINGLE WORD OF IT!" I was more than surprised to hear from some of them as I had not given the book to them directly. I even heard from a stake in Idaho asking if they could use the book throughout their stake one Christmas. These things warm a writer's heart. Thank you, and Go For It!

Of course, this little book does not have to be read at Christmas. Its simple chapter system is also designed so parents can read a chapter as a "good night" story to their children at any time of the year. *You will find the Christmasy parts in Italics to make them easier to skip over if you choose to.* Drifting minds filled with holy scripture or tales of the Restoration make for more pleasant dreams when bumps fill the night.

This little book is not, and never was, intended to be a comprehensive account of the Prophet's life and therefore does not contain every story, nor indeed, every important milestone. Instead, it is written to children and the young at heart, the kind mentioned in the *Gospel of Matthew*, eighteenth chapter, third verse. With this in mind, I have condensed, edited and clarified some of the grammar and stories. Those desiring more are encouraged to search out the best non-fiction accounts of Church History for themselves.

Some of these stories — particularly the early ones — are old favorites which you will remember and our children need to know, others are little known accounts. Thus, I hope there is something for everyone.

Lastly, because I can, I have included a reprint of the now infamous short booklet: *The Joseph Smith Daguerreotype. Was the Prophet Photographed* as a 25th anniversary bonus. It has originally written as a primer to explain the scientific facts behind the only photograph of the Prophet Joseph taken during his lifetime and authenticated by his own immediately family in the 1800s. It caused quite a controversy in its day, which was not my intention. It should be considered as a separate chapter on its own.

Happy testimony building or Merry Christmas and Happy Birthday, but most of all, Thank you Lord Jesus for sending us Brother Joseph. And thank you again for giving us modern prophets in unbroken succession ever since.

A painting of the Prophet Joseph Smith. The Prophet's wife Emma and his oldest son, Joseph III, said that this painting most closely resembled Joseph Smith because it closely resembled a photograph which they had of him. Today we have abundant evidence that this painting was made from that photograph, partially for the reason that artists were beginning to use photography, instead of sketches, as models for their paintings. *Original owned by the Community of Christ Church, Missouri. This image is in the Public Domain.*

Chapter One
What is a Prophet?
(December 1st)

This Christmastime we are going to do something different. We are going to spend a little time each night learning about a modern prophet of God.

A prophet is a teacher with a message from our Father in Heaven. There have been many great prophets. Have you heard of Moses, Nephi, and Jonah? These were ancient prophets but there are modern prophets just as great. Have you heard about the first of the modern prophets? His name was Joseph Smith.

Joseph Smith was born on December 23rd 1805 in the tiny town of Sharon, Vermont. His parents were named Joseph and Lucy. He had two older brothers and one older sister. They were not a rich family, but they worked hard together and did their best to make a living. The first story about the young Prophet you need to know, is also one of the most famous. It happened around his eighth birthday.

When Joseph was still a little boy, his family came down with typhus fever. We don't get typhus fever much anymore in the United States but in Joseph Smith's time it was a real problem. Typhus comes from fleas that live on rats, mice or other small farm mammals. When children get typhus they become very sick. They get headaches, chills, and pains all over. Young Joseph was just beginning to feel better, when suddenly a terrible pain seized him in his shoulder. His pain was so bad that his mother sent for a doctor. The doctor rubbed some salve on the boy's shoulder and left. Joseph suffered for two more weeks.

When the doctor came back, he found that Joseph was no better. He examined him again and this time found a large sore between his shoulder blades. When the doctor cut the sore open, a whole quart of liquid and puss poured out. Then, Joseph felt the pain shoot down into his leg.

After two more weeks of suffering, his leg began to swell up. Joseph's parents didn't know what to do. His mother would carry him around the house and try to comfort him. Soon she was worn out from worry and fatigue.

Joseph's older brother Hyrum asked if he might have a turn helping Joseph. Hyrum would take his brother's leg in his arms and squeeze it to make the pain more bearable. Somehow the squeezing helped but not for long. Each time the doctor came he would cut open Joseph's leg and that helped as well, but when the leg healed shut, the pain would return.

At last, it was discovered that the problem was in Joseph's bone. After many weeks, the doctor returned with more doctors. They took Joseph's parents aside, "There is nothing we can do to help young Joseph unless we cut off his leg."

Mother Smith was horrified. She made the doctors promise that they would first try to cut out the bad part of the bone and not cut off Joseph's whole leg. The head doctor agreed to try. He ordered the other doctors to tie Joseph down on the bed and give him some liquor to dull the pain. It was really going to hurt.

Little Joseph looked up at the doctor and said, "No, I will not touch one particle of liquor, neither will I be tied down; but I will tell you what I will do—I will have my father sit on the bed and hold me in his arms, and then I will do whatever is necessary in order to have the bone taken out."

Then Joseph looked at his mother and said, "Mother, I want you to leave the room, for I know you cannot bear to see me suffer so; father can stand it, but you have carried me so much, and watched over me so long, you are almost worn out." Then he started to cry and said, "Now, mother, promise me that you will not stay. The Lord will help me, and I shall get through it."

Even in terrible pain, Joseph was more concerned about his mother's feelings than his own. It would have been very easy for Joseph to be selfish but he was not that kind of a boy. This is a good lesson to remember.

Mother Smith promised her son that she would go outside. Once she had gone, the doctors cut into Joseph's bone and using a pair of pliers broke out the first bad piece. Joseph screamed so loud that his mother heard him out in the yard. She was so upset that she ran back into the house and opened the door. Joseph lay on the bed covered in sweat, blood pouring from his leg.

Joseph saw her and cried, "Oh, mother, go back, go back; I do not want you to come in —I will try to tough it out, if you will go away."

Even though it was a very painful operation, it was successful. Soon Joseph's leg healed and his family thanked their Father in Heaven for helping them through a terrible time of sickness.

Farm life was hard in Vermont and every time the family tried to make a living there, something stopped them. They didn't know it then, but our Heavenly Father wanted the family to move to New York State and a small town called Manchester. Nearby is a large hill called the Hill Cumorah. Remember this name. We will talk about this important hill soon.

It was not easy for the boy Joseph and his family to get to Manchester. Many people wonder why this would be? If God wanted them to go to Manchester, why wouldn't He just make it easy for them to get there? It is a good question. What do you think about that?

Chapter Two
Growing Up
(December 2ⁿᵈ)

In New York State there is a small town called Manchester. It is here that the story of our church really begins. The Smith family had now grown larger. Joseph had two older brothers, Alvin and Hyrum and one older sister Sophronia. He had three younger brothers, Samuel, Don Carlos and William and two younger sisters Catherine and Lucy. They built a log cabin and began to clear land to plant crops. It was really hard work to cut down the big trees and pull up the roots. A boy could get really strong working long hours clearing a field like that.

While the family was busy trying to clear their field, they worked odd jobs to make money. Father Smith opened a cake and root beer shop. Americans have always loved root beer and his shop was successful. He also sold gingerbread, pies and boiled eggs. The Smith boys would also work on other people's farms: gardening, harvesting and digging wells.

Mother Smith and the girls would do laundry and make homemade tablecloths and curtains for people's homes. It was hard work. Those who knew the Smith family loved them. Mother Smith was kind and god-fearing. People enjoyed visiting her home. Of Father Smith, it was said, "He was smarter than most men and had the appearance of having descended from royalty."

Young Joseph was a hard worker and natural leader. Many farmers asked his parents if he could work for them. It is said that whenever a farmer hired Joseph, the other boys on the farm worked harder.

One young girl who grew up near the Smith Family farm remembered that her father loved young Joseph and often hired him to work with his boys. She remembered going into the field on an afternoon to play in the corn rows while her brothers worked. When evening came she was too tired to walk home and cried because her brothers refused to carry her home. Joseph lifted her on his shoulders and took her back safely. Her father said Joseph was "the best help he had ever found." In fact he always chose the time to hoe his large field based on when Joseph could help out. He said that whenever the wild boys worked by themselves much time would be spent in arguing, quarreling, and ring fighting. However, when Joseph worked with them, the work went forward without interruption. People would later say, "there was never a truer, purer, nobler boy than [Joseph Smith]."

Joseph made many friends including a boy named Orrin Porter Rockwell. Porter would became almost as famous as young Joseph one day, but we will tell you more about Porter later. Joseph was strong for his age. None of his young friends could remember him ever losing at boyish games, nonetheless, they said, he was always a good sport and played fair.

One day, when still a boy (you were not considered a man until you turned sixteen) Joseph saw a large man hitting his wife for something she had done. Joseph was so upset that he grabbed the man and began to beat him up. It was a hard fight as the man was much bigger than Joseph, but Joseph couldn't stand bullies. He said, "I whipped [that man] till he said he had enough." A few nights later, Joseph was just coming home from an errand. He climbed up the front porch and opened the door when the family heard the BANG of a gun. A bullet zipped past Joseph's head. Quickly, he jumped into the house. His father and brothers rushed outside to catch the shooter but could find no trace of him in the darkness.

The next morning they found footprints under a wagon where the would-be murderer had been waiting. They found two bullets lodged in the head and neck of a cow that was standing opposite the wagon in a dark corner. The family never did discover who tried to kill Joseph that night. Was it the man that Joseph had humbled for beating his wife? We may never know the answer for sure.

A stump preacher giving a sermon to a group of townspeople who have gathered to hear him.

Chapter Three
One Last Commission
(December 3rd)

When Joseph was about fourteen years old, a great religious revival spread across America. A religious revival is simply a campaign to get people excited about joining a neighborhood church. The problem was each church wanted to get the most people to join their congregation. Each church would say that they were the right one and all the others were wrong.

Mother Smith decided that the family needed to pick a church. Father Smith thought the whole thing was nonsense, "I can take my Bible somewhere quiet, and study, and pray and learn more on my own than I can from any of these churches." Mother Smith thought differently. She said that a young family needed a minister and a weekly sermon to grow up straight and true. So, Mother Smith took the children to try out different churches, and Father Smith taught the children hymn singing and scripture reading at home. He told his children to make up their own minds in regards to which Christian church was best.

This was all very confusing to young Joseph. He wanted to join a church, but didn't know which one was best. At last he met a Methodist Minister named Reverend Lane. He told the minister how confused he was. The minister told Joseph to search the scriptures, pray, and follow his heart.

Joseph did read his scriptures. One night as he was studying his *Bible*, he read the *Book of James*. You all know the scripture. It reads: "If any of you lack wisdom, let him ask of God, that giveth to all men liberally, and upbraideth not; and it shall be given him."

These may seem like big words but they simply mean that "If you want to know what God wants you to do, ask him, and he will tell you. He won't be mad or upset that you asked him, no matter what." Isn't that great to know?

Joseph thought a lot about that scripture. He decided to give it a try. He went to a quiet grove of trees near his house and offered a prayer. You know what happened; our Heavenly Father and His Son, Jesus Christ, the Savior of the world, appeared. They told Joseph that he was not to join any church. They said that someday they would restore the true church of Christ and that Joseph could help them do it.

Joseph was so excited! He had prayed to God and God had answered him. Joseph also learned that God the Father and Jesus Christ were two separate heavenly men. This is very important to know. Many people think that God the Father and his Son, Jesus Christ, are somehow, in a mysterious way, just one person. Isn't that a silly thing? Every school boy knows that a boy can't be his own father, but that is just what the ministers were teaching young Joseph. He also learned that God loved His children very much. So much, in fact, that He was going to bring the true church back to earth again.

Joseph couldn't wait to tell everyone the good news. But, what do you think happened? Were people excited to hear about Joseph's vision? No, they were not! Even Joseph's minister friend, who told him that praying would help him find an answer was angry. He said, "God doesn't speak to man any more, Joseph. If you saw anything at all in the woods, it was the devil."

Joseph was shocked. Very quickly the word spread all around town. Joseph learned he had to be careful what he said, but his family believed him. That made all the difference.

It seemed to Joseph that everything changed overnight. Where once his family had been well respected, now terrible lies were being spread about them everywhere. Joseph was teased constantly. People called him, "Old Holy Joe!" He could hardly go anywhere alone. Once his father sent him into town to have a horse shod and before long a crowd had formed around him. "Say, young Joe," they mocked, "tell us of that remarkable vision you had when an angel appeared to you with glad tidings of great joy!"

"Yeah!" another taunted, "Old Holy Joe! Ain't you a pure one. Did the holy one really say that all your sins had been forgiven?"

And even the local pastor, who was supposed to be full of Christian kindness, said, "Yeah, your Highness, tell the Lord to hurry up and let us know which parts of the Bible ain't true."

People didn't want Joseph to work for them anymore. They were afraid that other boys might believe his story. One churchman told a neighbor, "The influence that boy carries is a danger for the coming generation, not only the young men but all that meet him will follow him, and he must be put down!"

One of the young men who believed Joseph was Porter Rockwell. One day Porter and Joseph rode into town together. On the outskirts of town, eight men jumped them.

"Hold on, boys," one said, "Port, you ain't fit company for the Smith boy, fer he has seen God. Ain't that so, Joe?"

As the men laughed, one of the gang, Dick Williams, looked Joseph in the eye, "Your story is a lie, Joe, and you know it."

Joseph straightened up and said, "Sir, it is not a lie. I have seen a vision."

George Cuyler suddenly yelled, "Yank that lying brat off that horse and let's choke them blasphemous lies outta his throat."

Williams grabbed Joseph, but Porter struck him with the butt of his horse whip. Then, the gang jumped them. Joseph was seized by his hair as the men yanked him from the horse.

One of them yelled, "Let's drown the dirty liar, then he won't tell anymore whoppers."

The men carried the struggling Joseph to a large pond and threw him in. Joseph sank into the water. As he came up sputtering, one of the ruffians yelled: "Now, Joe, will you deny that story?"

Joseph balancing himself in the pond replied, "I have seen a vision, I know it and God knows it. I cannot deny it, or I would offend God."

"That's it!" the men cried, diving into the water, "Let's drown the liar and do God a favor."

As the men raced in to hold Joseph under, suddenly the sound of a wagon coming down the road was heard. The men were afraid of having someone witness their murderous deed and so they let Joseph go and ran off into the woods.

Another time a big, burly man stopped the young prophet on the street and got right in his face accusing him of being a terrible liar. "If you met anyone in the woods that day, it was the devil," he said. Quick as lightening, Joseph hit the man right between the eyes. The big bully fell to the ground and never bothered the young boy again.

Chapter Four
A Golden Book from a Warrior Prophet
(December 4th)

Nearly four years had passed since Joseph had seen his First Vision and, while lots of people had made fun of him and some had tried to hurt him, Joseph had heard nothing from God about what part he was to play in bringing the true church back to earth. Many people in town had forgotten about Joseph's First Vision, or they didn't care anymore. Even one of Joseph's friends had decided that Joseph had received a sweet dream and that it was not important. Joseph Smith, on the other hand, knew that his First Vision was very important and began to worry that maybe God wasn't going to use him after all. Joseph also felt guilty because since his First Vision, he had had to fight bullies. Joseph thought that fighting was a sin. He felt bad about some of the things he had done. On the night of September 21st, 1823, he decided it was time to repent and ask God again what he should do.

Joseph waited until his family was asleep, then he knelt down and prayed. Soon the room was filled with a brilliant light and an angel appeared. Joseph would later say:

He had on a loose robe of most exquisite whiteness. It was a whiteness beyond anything earthly I had ever seen... his whole person was glorious beyond description, and his countenance truly like lightning... When I first looked upon him, I was afraid; but the fear soon left me. He called me by name, and said unto me that he was a messenger sent from the presence of God to me, and that his name was Moroni; that God had a work for me to do...

Next time you look at one of our temples, take a moment and look closely at the beautiful golden statue of the Angel Moroni on the top tower. When you see these statues of Moroni, you are supposed to remember this wonderful story about how God sent the Angel Moroni to the Prophet Joseph. The statue is suppose to remind you that the true church of God has been returned to the earth.

Have you heard of the Golden Plates? It is a wonderful story. It is so wonderful because it is true. The Angel Moroni told Joseph that many years go, before George Washington and even before Christopher Columbus, God told a prophet named Lehi to leave his home in Jerusalem and travel with his family and friends to the Americas. When they arrived in the Americas, Lehi's family split into two groups. Those who chose to follow Satan called themselves Lamanites, but those who wanted to follow God called themselves Nephites.

The Nephites and the Lamanites had many wars, sometimes the Lamanites won and sometimes the Nephites won. There was even a time when the Lamanites became good and the Nephites became evil. All in all, these early American peoples learned that when they trusted in God, and kept his commandments, they were happy. When they did not, they suffered terribly. The most exciting story on the Golden Plates told about the visit of Jesus Christ to America. He taught them to love one another and established His true church among the people. It is a wonderful story. In the end, the people forgot the Lord and killed each other. Their last great leader was a man named Mormon. He wrote the history of his people on golden plates and called it the *Book of Mormon.*

A long time ago, his son Moroni buried these Golden Plates in the very hill where their last great battle took place, the Hill Cumorah, not far from Joseph Smith's home. This great General's son, now an angel, told Joseph that if he would be faithful, God would use him as the means of translating these Golden Plates into English so that we could read them.

Moroni told the young prophet that there were two stones set in silver bows, similar to a pair of glasses—and these stones, fastened to a breastplate, were known anciently as the *Urim and Thummim*. Any man who had this wonderful tool in his possession was called a seer and a prophet. God would give these to Joseph so that he could translate the *Book of Mormon* into English. This *Book of Mormon*, together with the *Holy Bible*, would give a complete picture of the gospel of Jesus Christ and would be the means of saving many of God's children. Joseph was told where the plates were hidden and how to find them.

The next day, Joseph walked to the Hill Cumorah. He would later say that along the walk, he felt two forces pulling on his mind. One force was good and holy and told him that the Lord would help him translate the book. Many people would learn the truth from the *Book of Mormon*. The other force whispered that the plates were made of gold. They were very valuable and, since Joseph's family was poor, there might be some way of using the plates to become rich.

When Joseph reached the place where the plates were hidden, he discovered a rounded rock. He pried it up and found that it was the lid to a stone box. The box was large enough that a breast plate could sit on the bottom. On top of this breast plate were three small cement pillars on which sat the Golden Plates.

As he gazed at the holy record, his mind thought for a moment about the great wealth that lay before him. Joseph reached in to take the precious plates when suddenly he was shocked by a powerful force that drained away his strength. Joseph tried again and this time was shocked even more forcefully. Confused, Joseph tried a third time, and the shock so completely drained his strength that he could barely move. Joseph cried out, "Why can I not obtain this book?"

"Because you have not kept the commandments of the Lord," answered a voice nearby. Joseph turned to look and saw the Angel Moroni standing by him. Moroni told the young man that his heart had to be pure if he was to obtain the plates. Moroni pointed out into the distance and told Joseph to look as a vision opened. Joseph saw the devil and millions of his helpers, they were dark, ugly, and full of sinful desires. They made Joseph feel sad, greedy, and sneaky. They whispered that the plates were very valuable and could make Joseph rich. Then Moroni showed Joseph the glory of God, brilliant, beautiful, and full of goodness. It made Joseph feel strong, good, and noble. Moroni told Joseph that he must never forget the difference between these two forces and how they made him feel. God wants us to do good things, but Satan only wants us to be selfish and sinful.

Moroni finished by saying that Joseph was not to take the plates just yet. He needed more time to prepare himself. He was to come back to this spot each year, and when he was ready, God would let him have them. Joseph had learned a valuable lesson. He had seen the difference between the power of God and the trickery of the devil. Joseph would later tell his friends that this experience was very beneficial for him as it taught him how to tell which voice, God's or the devil's, was speaking to his mind. It would be several more years before Joseph was permitted to take the plates.

During that time, Joseph was taught by Moroni personally and by the Lord through dreams at night. Often he would tell his family about what he had learned. His older brother Alvin loved to hear Joseph talk about the ancient Americans. Many farmers and other people had found the ruins of old forts, rusty swords, and weapons about their farms near the Hill Cumorah. No one knew the history of what had happened there until Joseph revealed the mystery.

It was also during this time that Joseph was hired by a family friend named Josiah Stoal to help him search for a silver mine which the Spaniards were supposed to have hidden in Pennsylvania. Needing the money and work, Joseph agreed. While searching unsuccessfully for the mine, he met and married a beautiful woman named Emma Hale. Emma's parents had heard about Joseph's visions and weren't happy that Emma wanted to marry the young prophet, but she married him anyway.

An old engraving from 1841 of "Mormon's Hill" called Cumorah by the Nephites in the *Book of Mormon*. It is located in Upstate New York near the city of Manchester.

Chapter Five
The Book of Mormon
America's Testimony of Jesus Christ
(December 5th)

After four years of waiting and preparing his mind and heart, the Lord allowed Joseph to take the Golden Plates from their secret hiding place in the stone box on the Hill Cumorah. Moroni had warned Joseph that people would try to steal them from him. Many people did try.

Joseph didn't have the plates long when his father and brothers were hired to work on a rich man's farm. The man was named Martin Harris. Martin was very interested in Joseph's First Vision. While Father Smith and Hyrum were walling a basement and digging a well for Mr. Harris, he asked them many questions. Each day while they were there, Martin would find an excuse to quiz them about Joseph.

Finally, one day Father Smith told Martin all about Joseph's wonderful experiences with the Angel Moroni and the Golden Plates. Martin was thrilled! He wanted to know everything and promised to keep it a secret. But Martin was terrible at keeping secrets, and soon everyone knew that Joseph had a fortune in gold.

It was not long before everyone wanted Joseph's Golden Plates. Even Martin Harris, who believed Joseph, gathered a group of men together and went to the Hill Cumorah with some tools to search for more plates and treasure. Martin later said, "I will tell you a wonderful thing that happened after Joseph had found the plates. Three of us took some tools to go to the hills and hunt for some more boxes, or gold, or something, and indeed we found a stone box. We got quite excited about it, and dug around it carefully, and we were ready to take it up, but behold it slipped back into the hill. We stood there and looked at it and one of us took a crowbar and tried to drive it through the lid to hold it, but it glanced and broke one corner off the box." The box disappeared back into the hill, and they could not get hold of it.

One day, Joseph came running into the house looking very concerned. He asked his mother if any men had been wandering about. When she said no, he replied that a mob would come looking for the plates that night.

Immediately, Joseph asked his family to help him remove a portion of the fireplace and bury the plates and Urim and Thummim beneath it. They had scarcely replaced the hearth when a large body of men, with guns, came rushing at the house.

Joseph threw open the door and, pretending to have a whole army of men inside, ordered a charge on the mob. All the men of the family, from the father down to little Carlos, ran out of the house with such fury that the mob was struck with terror. They fled into the woods, defeated. Joseph had learned this trick from the stories his mother told him. Her father, Solomon Mack, had fought bravely in the Revolutionary War and had once done the same thing to scare away a band of Indians.

A short time later, Joseph received another revelation that the mob was coming back and that the plates were not safe under the fireplace. Quickly, Joseph took them out of the box in which they were hidden, and wrapping them in clothes, carried them across the road to a cooper's shop. There, he hid them in a bunch of flax which was piled in the shop loft. After which he nailed the empty box shut, tore up the floor of the shop, and put the box underneath.

As soon as night came, the mob ransacked the place. They rummaged around the house and all over the premises. The next morning the Smiths found the floor of the cooper's shop torn up and the empty box smashed open. The family was amazed. A few days later they learned that an evil young woman was using a magic crystal to ask the devil where "Joe Smith kept his Gold Bible hid." She had seen the box under the shop floor but didn't know that Joseph had hidden the plates elsewhere.

Another time, Joseph's sisters were working about the house when Joseph came running up to a window and thrust a bundle through at Catherine telling her to hide it quickly. Sophronia helped her hide it under their corn husk mattress. Then, the two girls got into bed and pretended to be asleep. No sooner had they laid down when an angry mob broke into the house and began searching through everything looking for the package. When they opened the girls' bedroom, the mob saw the girls sleeping so peacefully. They decided not to wake them. Thus, these brave little girls saved the Golden Plates!

There are many stories like these, but Joseph was faithful to the Lord's commandments and so was always one step ahead of the mobs. All this chaos made it impossible for Joseph to translate the plates. He decided to take his wife Emma back to her parent's home in Pennsylvania and get some peace.

In Pennsylvania, Joseph was able to start translating the Golden Plates into what today we call the *Book of Mormon*. Joseph had several scribes help him, including Emma.

Joseph would set up a sheet for a screen across a table. He would sit on one side with the Golden Plates and his scribe would sit on the other side. He had been commanded not to show the plates to any one without God's permission. It took a lot of faith for Joseph and his scribes to keep this rule, but it was important since the plates could not be translated without faith. After the scribe was in position, Joseph would then strap the breast plate onto his chest and hook the wonderful glasses, called the Urim and Thummim, into a hole in the breast plate. This left Joseph's hands free to turn the golden pages.

Joseph would look at the plates through the lens of the Urim and Thummim and concentrate on the strange writing. Then, inside his mind he would see the characters with their English letters beneath. When it was correct Joseph would feel a warm feeling inside, and he would read or spell out what he saw to his scribe who would write it down. It was slow work at first. Poor Emma had so much housework to do, along with being Joseph's scribe. It was too much for her. It was not long before the Lord sent Martin Harris to help.

Martin said that he would help Joseph with money and other needs if he could get some assurance that Joseph was telling the truth about the Golden Plates. The Lord told Joseph to copy down some of the characters on the plates and give them to Martin to take to New York City, to a famous professor named Charles Anthon of Columbia University. He was known as America's foremost classicist, having published fifty textbooks on the subject of ancient societies.

Martin did take the characters to Professor Anthon. According to Martin, Professor Anthon was fascinated with them, stating that they seemed to be some form of Egyptian writing but that he could not read them. When Professor Anthon asked Martin where he got the characters, Martin told him the wonderful story of Joseph Smith and the Angel Moroni. Professor Anthon didn't believe the story and sent Martin away. This meeting so affected Martin that he agreed to help Joseph translate and publish the manuscript. It also fulfilled an ancient prophecy by the great poet-prophet Isaiah. (see Isaiah 29:9-14)

While Martin Harris was showing the characters to men in New York, Joseph asked Emma to be his scribe again. While they were translating the first chapter known as the *Book of Lehi*, Joseph came upon a passage describing Jerusalem as a city surrounded by walls.

Joseph stopped translating and turned to Emma, "Did Jerusalem have walls around it?"

When she answered yes, he was greatly relieved. Joseph had never seen a wall that went around an entire city. It seemed incredible to him, coming from the open farmlands of America, that a big city could have a wall that went all the way around it. Emma would later tell that story to show people that Joseph did not have enough education nor experience to make up anything as complicated as the *Book of Mormon*.

Emma remembered this about their translating together:

When my husband was translating the Book of Mormon, I wrote a part of it, as he dictated each sentence, word for word, and when he came to proper names he could not pronounce, or long words, he spelled them out, and while I was writing them, if I made a mistake in spelling, although it was impossible for him to see how I was writing them down at the time, [he would correct me.] Even the word — Sarah — he could not pronounce at first, but had to spell it, and I would pronounce it for him. When he stopped for any purpose at any time he would, when he commenced again, begin where he left off without any hesitation...

Martin Harris returned from New York and helped Joseph again, but Martin's heart was not right with the Lord. Despite all that Martin had seen, he would, from time-to-time, test Joseph just to make certain he was still a Prophet. Along with the Urim & Thummim, the Lord had also given Joseph several stones which he could use when it was not practical to use the larger Urim & Thummim with its heavy breastplate. These were called Seer Stones, but worldly people sometimes call them *Philosopher Stones*. Many ancient prophets used them, including the High Priests of Israel under Moses and under Kings David and Solomon. They are one of the signs of a true prophet.

The Lord had commanded Joseph to never show the Golden Plates or the Urim & Thummim to anyone without specific permission first. This was important because the gifts of God cannot work without faith. It took faith for anyone supporting Joseph's mission to help him. This faith was very important. It was also a sacrifice for Joseph too. Satan has no power when people have faith and are willing to sacrifice something. Also, the gift of the Holy Ghost had not yet been returned to the Earth, so Joseph's only power at first was faith and sacrifice. It took great faith to translate the plates and not let anyone else see them. You and I are very blessed today to be given the gift of the Holy Ghost after we are baptized. The Holy Ghost gives boys and girls great power over Satan. This power gives us comfort and safety and even makes us smarter since the Holy Ghost can help us remember things when we need them. It really bothered Martin that he was not allowed to see the Golden Plates or the Urim & Thummim. Martin did not have a lot of faith at times. Martin was allowed to see the Seer Stones. Using them made translating easier on Joseph when he did not have a private place to bring out the plates and the Urim & Thummim.

People would often interrupt Joseph's work. Sometimes innocently, but other times on purpose hoping to steal the Golden Plates or Urim & Thummim.

Also, if it was too bright outside, sometimes Joseph would put one of these stones in a hat and then place his face into the rim to block out the light. When the Lord was ready, he would make the stone glow and Joseph could then translate the plates through the stone. During one particular translation session, after a short break, Martin found a regular rock and switched it with Joseph's stone when the young prophet wasn't looking. When they returned to their work, Joseph placed his face in the hat and after many minutes, he lifted his face up and, with deep concern turned to Martin and said, "I don't know what's wrong. All is dark and I can't translate anything." A wide smile crossed Martin's face and he told Joseph that he had tricked him. When Joseph asked him why, Martin said, "I just wanted to make sure you could really do it."

Poor Joseph. Even today some people make fun of the Lord and His young prophet because they think using a Urim & Thummim or Seer Stone in a hat is a silly way to translate a book of scripture. But the really silly thing is that these are the same people who think it's really neat for God to send a huge fish to swallow the Prophet Jonah, or for Him to divide the ocean for Moses and the Ancient Israelites, but who don't believe that God uses miracles today. They also think that if God does choose to perform a miracle, He had better do it their way. Don't you be so silly. Remember that it takes faith to please God. It doesn't take very much faith to do something you already think makes perfect sense. Sometimes God wants to see if you have enough faith to trust Him and just do something His way.

Martin also had a nasty wife who wanted to stop Joseph's prophetic mission. You probably already know the story of how Martin's wife stole the first chapter of the *Book of Mormon*, known as the *Book of Lehi*, after it was translated. And, how, eventually the Lord fired Martin Harris as Joseph's scribe and then placed an appendix known as the *Book of Nephi* in place of the *Book of Lehi*. Without Martin's help, Joseph needed a new scribe to help him finish the book. The Lord had just the person in mind.

Oliver Cowdery, the second Elder and only "Vice-President" of the Church. Oliver witnessed many angelic and miraculous events. He stands as a witness to the truthfulness of Joseph Smith's early accounts. It has been a puzzlement to Mormonism's enemies that even after Oliver left the church over conflicts with Joseph Smith, he continued to state until his death that everything he had witnessed with Joseph Smith really happened. Many years after the death of the Prophet Joseph, Oliver asked Brigham Young to reinstate his membership in the Church now based in Salt Lake City, Utah. He died in the faith.

Chapter Six
Oliver Cowdery
(December 6th)

After the Lord fired Martin Harris, Joseph needed a new scribe, and the Lord had the perfect man in mind. In the Spring of 1829, a young school teacher moved into the area and heard the story of Joseph Smith. His name was Oliver Cowdery. Oliver believed the story and wanted to help Joseph translate the plates. Joseph was grateful for Oliver's help, since Oliver was very good at grammar and spelling. This made the translation go much faster. Joseph and Oliver worked many long hours together. You can get a feeling for how smart Oliver was by reading some of the accounts of his days with Joseph. Oliver wrote, "These were days never to be forgotten — to sit under the sound of a voice dictated by the inspiration of heaven, awakened the utmost gratitude of this bosom! Day after day I continued, uninterrupted, to write from his mouth, as he translated with the Urim and Thummim, or, as the Nephites would have said, Interpreters, the history or record called The Book of Mormon..."

These are beautiful words. They show you how well Oliver knew how to use the English language.

As translation of the *Book of Mormon* continued, the men came to a place where the plates spoke of the importance of being baptized. Jesus had said that no one could enter heaven without being baptized. As Joseph and Oliver puzzled about this, they were given a commandment from heaven to go to a nearby river.

Eagerly the two men hurried to the river and there along the banks, Oliver met his first Angel. It was the Angel John the Baptist. You will remember how John the Baptist was Jesus's cousin and how he had baptized Jesus "in the river Jordan's flow." Well, this very same John the Baptist returned to Earth with the authority to baptize in Jesus's name. We call this authority the Aaronic Priesthood. The Angel John the Baptist placed his hands on Joseph's and Oliver's heads and gave them the Aaronic Priesthood and told them to go into the water and baptize each other.

You will discover in your life that every time God gives you a special blessing, Satan takes an opportunity to tempt you. This is part of the law of opposition, and it is never fun to go through. But if you know that Satan will tempt you after a special blessing from God, you can be ready. When the trial comes you can say in your heart, "I know that this trial will not last long." You should remember that the very fact that doubts and trials do come is proof that the gospel is true, since God warned you ahead of time that it would happen.

Since the Lord had given Joseph and Oliver such a wonderful gift as baptism and the Aaronic Priesthood, it meant that Satan would get his turn to make things difficult. Soon a mob began to threaten Joseph's life again. At first Joseph's father-in-law was able to keep them away, but not for long.

One day, as Joseph was translating the plates with the Urim and Thummim, he received a commandment to write a letter to a young man named David Whitmer, who lived in Waterloo, New York. He was to ask David to hurry and come with his horses, and move Joseph, Emma and Oliver to his father's house for safety. Joseph was told that an evil gang of men were going to try and kill them. Joseph quickly wrote the letter. When David Whitmer received it, he showed it to his father and asked him what he should do.

Mr. Whitmer told his son that he could not go until his chores were finished. He had at least two days of wheat to plant and a lot of plaster to sow. His father told him not to go unless he could get an answer from God that it really was important.

David did pray and felt a voice in his mind say, "Go as soon as your wheat is planted."

The next morning David woke up early and got to work. To his great surprise, he discovered that at the end of one day, he had done two days of work. Now, this is impossible. When his father saw this, he said, "There must be an overruling hand in this, and I think you had better go down to Pennsylvania as soon as your plaster of Paris is sown."

The next morning, David took a wooden measure under his arm and went out to sow the plaster, which he had left in a heap near his sister's house. When he got to where the plaster was, he discovered it was gone! He ran to his sister, and asked of her if she knew what had happened to his plaster. She told him that it was all sown the day before. That was impossible, David told her.

"I am astonished at that," replied his sister, "for the children came to me in the forenoon, and begged of me to go out and see the men sow plaster in the field, saying, that they never saw anybody sow plaster so fast in their lives. I accordingly went, and saw three men at work in the field, as the children said, but, supposing that you had hired some help, on account of your hurry, I left them be." David immediately left with his horse team to rescue Joseph and bring them safely to his house.

There are two other wonderful true stories about David Whitmer coming to rescue Joseph, which I want you to know. Joseph, as a prophet, had the power of prophecy; this means that he could see the future and events that happened far away. Joseph prophesized to Oliver everything that David would do during the journey to come and get them. Oliver was astonished. He wrote down everything that Joseph said. Things like: "David left home on such a day, and he drove to such a place and there watered his horses, ate his lunch, then drove to another such place." Joseph gave a perfect description of what David did all along the way. Right down to the tavern sign that he read along the road. He even told Oliver the exact time that David would arrive.

Sure enough, at that very time Oliver Cowdery stole away and went out to meet David. When they met, Oliver took David aside and said, "Joseph has told me so and so; you left home at such a time, and stopped at such a place," and then went on to describe David's entire journey.

David said, "How did Joseph know?"

Oliver replied, "I do not know, but that is what he told me."

David remarked that if the Prophet had been with him and traveled every foot of the way, he could not have told the facts more correctly.

It didn't take Joseph, Emma and Oliver long to pack. During the journey something amazing happened. All of a sudden, in the middle of a prairie, there appeared a man walking along the road. David said he raised his hat and rubbed his brow, as if he were a little warm, and said, "Good morning."

Oliver and David looked at each other and began to marvel and wonder: "Where did this man come from?" David described him as having an old-fashioned knapsack on his back. He was carrying something of considerable weight. They turned to Joseph, "What does it mean?"

Joseph said, "Ask him to ride."

When they did. The man said, "No, I am just going over to Cumorah."

David said, "Cumorah? What is Cumorah?" He had never heard of Cumorah, and he thought he knew the country very well. While David was looking around and trying to ascertain what the mystery was, the man disappeared. This disturbed David and he demanded of Joseph, "What does this mean?"

Joseph informed him that the man was Moroni, and that the bundle on his back contained the Golden Plates which Joseph had delivered to him before they departed. Moroni was taking them for safety, and would return them when they reached the Whitmer's home. The journey was a safe one, but when they arrived at the Whitmer house, David's mother was not happy about having more people to feed.

Women worked very hard. In those days, there were no dish washers, vacuums, or grocery stores to make life easier. She felt down-hearted and discouraged when she saw Joseph. How was she going to provide for her own family plus more? She went down to milk the cow feeling gloomy. David said that when she came back she was full of joy. Her son didn't understand what had changed her heart so quickly. She happily welcomed Joseph, Emma, and Oliver into their home.

When David asked her what had changed her mind, she said that she had seen Moroni. She then described the very same man that David had seen walking on the prairies with a knapsack. She said Moroni told her that Joseph had come to her home for safety and he was in her care and protection. He told her that her burdens would be lightened, and she would enjoy her service, and not to be bowed down with sorrow. Then he opened a box and showed her the Golden Plates. David said after that she was the happiest woman in the world for she knew that Joseph was a true prophet.

Now some people will say, why did she get to see the plates and others did not? If you will stop and think about it for a minute, the answer will come to you.

Chapter Seven
Witnesses to the Latter-day Work
(December 7th)

At the Whitmer home, Joseph was able to finish translating the Golden Plates. Oliver was told to make a complete second copy of the manuscript. While reading the book, they came upon a scripture in Ether 5:2-4 which reads, "And behold, ye may be privileged that ye may show the plates unto those who shall assist to bring forth this work;… And in the mouth of three witnesses shall these things be established…and all this shall stand as a testimony against the world at the last day."

Oliver Cowdery, David Whitmer, and Martin Harris wanted to be these three witnesses. The next morning, Joseph, Martin, Oliver, and David went into a grove, a short distance from the house, and started to pray. Soon an angel appeared and showed them the Golden Plates and the Urim and Thummim. The Angel lifted the plates and turned the pages over in his hands. Then he allowed the men to hold them, study them and turn the pages themselves. The angel told the men that the *Book of Mormon* was correctly translated by the power of God. It contained the fullness of the gospel of Jesus Christ to the Nephites. He then told the men that they were required to bear testimony of these things, and of this open vision, to the people of the world. The men wrote up an official statement called the Testimony of the Three Witnesses. It reads, in part:

> Be it known unto all nations, kindreds, tongues, and people, unto whom this work shall come: That we, through the grace of God the Father, and our Lord Jesus Christ, have seen the plates which contain this record, which is a

record of the people of Nephi, and also of the Lamanites, their brethren, and also of the people of Jared, who came from the tower of which hath been spoken. And we also know that they have been translated by the gift and power of God, for his voice hath declared it unto us; wherefore we know of a surety that the work is true. And we also testify that we have seen the engravings which are upon the plates; and they have been shown unto us by the power of God, and not of man. And we declare with words of soberness, that an angel of God came down from heaven, and he brought and laid before our eyes, that we beheld and saw the plates, and the engravings thereon; and we know that it is by the grace of God the Father, and our Lord Jesus Christ, that we beheld and bear record that these things are true. And it is marvelous in our eyes. Nevertheless, the voice of the Lord commanded us that we should bear record of it; wherefore, to be obedient unto the commandments of God, we bear testimony of these things. And we know that if we are faithful in Christ, we shall rid our garments of the blood of all men, and be found spotless before the judgment-seat of Christ, and shall dwell with him eternally in the heavens. And the honor be to the Father, and to the Son, and to the Holy Ghost, which is one God. Amen.   (signed)

Oliver Cowdery

David Whitmer

Martin Harris

Afterwards, Joseph was so happy. He returned to his parents and said, "Father, Mother, you do not know how happy I am. The Lord has now caused the plates to be shown to three more besides myself. They have seen an angel, who has testified to them, and they will have to bear witness to the truth of what I have said, for now they know for themselves, that I do not go about to deceive the people, and I feel as if I was relieved of a burden which was almost too heavy for me to bear, and it rejoices my soul, that I am not any longer to be entirely alone in the world."

A short time after these three men received their powerful witness of the *Book of Mormon*, eight other men, including the Prophet's father and brothers Hyrum and Samuel were also given the privilege of seeing and holding the Golden Plates. Although some of the witnesses later left the church, none of them ever denied that they had seen the Golden Plates and an angel from heaven.

Remember this story the next time someone tells you that the *Book of Mormon* is not true and that Joseph Smith made the whole thing up and other ridiculous things like that. You can tell them the story of the witnesses and ask them to explain how they could have seen a angel and felt the Golden Plates if it were not true.

A short time later the *Book of Mormon* was published in Palmyra, New York. Martin Harris mortgaged his farm for $3,000 in order to pay the printing bill. Joseph and Oliver were made Elders in the Melchizedek Priesthood, and many other wonderful things happened. After Joseph was finished with the Golden Plates, he was commanded to return them to Moroni for safety. Brigham Young tells us what happened to them:

I believe that I will take the liberty to tell you... an incident in the life of Oliver Cowdery... I tell these things to you, and I have a motive for doing so. I want to carry them to the ears of my brethren and sisters, and to the children also, that they may grow to an understanding of some things that seem to be entirely hidden from the human family. Oliver Cowdery went with the Prophet Joseph when he [returned the plates to Cumorah. When they arrived there], the hill opened, and they walked into a cave, in which there was a large and spacious room. He says he did not think, at the time, whether they had the light of the sun or artificial light; but that it was just as light as day [inside]. They laid the plates on a table... Under this table there was a pile of plates as much as two feet high, and there were altogether in this room more plates than probably many wagon loads; they were piled up in the corners and along the walls.

The first time they went there the sword of Laban hung upon the wall; but when they went again, it had been taken down and laid upon the table across the gold plates; it was unsheathed, and on it was written these words "This sword will never be sheathed again until the kingdoms of this world become the kingdoms of our God and his Christ." ...Now, you may think I am unwise in publicly telling these things, thinking perhaps I should preserve them in my own breast; but such is not my mind. I would like the people called Latter-day Saints to understand some little things with regard to the workings and dealings of the Lord with his people here upon the earth. I could relate to you a great many more...

Chapter Eight
The Church of Jesus Christ of Latter-day Saints
(December 8th)

In a few days it will be December 23rd. This is an important day to our people because it was the birthday of Joseph Smith, but there is another date that is even more important. It is April 6th. The Lord was very clear with the young prophet that on April 6th 1830, those men who had witnessed the truthfulness of the *Book of Mormon* were to officially re-organize God's true church on the earth. Joseph was told that April 6th was so important because it was the actual birth date of Jesus Christ nearly two thousand years ago.

On the Lord's birthday, about sixty people met at the log home of Peter Whitmer. Joseph asked six of the men if they would fill the legal requirements for forming a new church. They agreed. Joseph led them in prayer and afterward asked those in attendance if they would accept him and Oliver as their spiritual leaders. Everyone raised their hand to vote yes. They had a sacrament meeting and afterward Father and Mother Smith, Martin Harris, Porter Rockwell and others went outside to be baptized.

The *Book of Mormon* promises that if a person reads it with an open mind, they can pray to God and ask Him if it is true. The new church sent missionaries out with the *Book of Mormon* into the countryside. Many of the great names you have heard about in Church History purchased or borrowed a copy of this new book of scripture and became convinced of the truthfulness of the restored church. Famous names like Brigham Young, W.

W. Phelps, and Parley P. Pratt joined the young church, but you remember before that we learned about the law of opposition. Satan couldn't stand by and just let the Lord's restored church take over the whole area. Oh, no, it was not long before people were complaining about the missionaries, Joseph Smith and the *Book of Mormon*. Preachers complained that doing missionary work was disturbing the peace and Joseph had to go to court. But none of this really caused too much trouble until one day Joseph received a letter from Oliver Cowdery, who had been living with the Whitmer Family.

Joseph had been busy arranging and making copies of the revelations he had received when Oliver wrote to the prophet that he had found a mistake in one of Joseph's revelations. Oliver said that it contained bad doctrine and should be removed from the scripture. Joseph was shocked. The young Prophet also learned that Oliver had convinced others that the revelation needed to be changed. It was only with some difficulty that Joseph was able to convince them that the revelation was correct as written since it was given by God, Himself.

Joseph had just gotten past that problem when another one surfaced. Another member of the church, a man named Hiram Page, had found a seer-stone which he claimed allowed him to receive revelation for the church that was just as good as Joseph Smith's.

It was due to these experiences that the Lord gave a revelation which every church member needs to understand. It is found in *Doctrine & Covenants 28*; it says that only the President of the whole church can receive revelation from God for the whole church. This is very important.

While it is true that personal revelation is a correct principle of the gospel, a man or woman will only receive revelation from God for the stewardship he or she has charge over. For example, the Holy Ghost might help you write a Primary talk, or tell your father something important that the Lord wants you to know. The bishop in your ward could get a revelation for his ward, or, your mother might receive a revelation to help her child, but your mom will never receive a revelation telling the bishop what to do. You will never receive a revelation telling the prophet what to say at General Conference. If you remember this, then someday when Satan puts a thought into your mind about what someone is supposed to do, and you are not responsible for that person, you will not be deceived into thinking that the idea came from God, and that, that person had better listen to you.

A few months later, Joseph received a revelation that Oliver Cowdery was to take Peter Whitmer Jr., Ziba Peterson, and Parley P. Pratt and go to the American Indians. They were to preach the gospel to them and tell them about the *Book of Mormon*. Emma Smith and some of the sisters in the church worked long hours making warm clothing for these missionaries. With winter coming on, they began a 1,500 mile walk to teach the children of the Lamanites about their ancestors in the *Book of Mormon*.

The first tribe they found was the friendly Seneca Indians who lived near Buffalo, New York. The Indians were very interested and thanked the men for the copies of the *Book of Mormon* they gave them. Then the missionaries trekked westward toward Lake Erie and the Ohio Valley.

Along the way, Parley P. Pratt told his fellow missionaries that he had a minister friend living in the area named Sidney Rigdon. They decided to stop and preach the restored gospel to Sidney.

Sidney was very interested in the gospel and promised that he would read the *Book of Mormon*. The missionaries next asked if they might be allowed to preach the same message in Sidney's church. He agreed. Soon it seemed that everyone was interested in the gospel. The missionaries next went to the nearby town of Kirtland where they preached from door to door. In just three weeks, 127 people were baptized, and the church had doubled in size.

The missionaries continued westward to the small frontier town of Independence, Missouri; then on to Indian Territory. There they found Chief Anderson of the Delaware tribe. The chief was very interested in the missionaries' message and invited 40 other tribal leaders to his lodge to hear Oliver Cowdery speak.

Oliver gave a masterful sermon. He said, "Thousands of moons ago, when the red men's forefathers dwelt in peace and possessed this whole land, the Great Spirit talked with them, and revealed His law and His will, and much knowledge to their wise men and prophets." Oliver told them that their great prophets had written all their ancient history and prophecies in a golden book. This book told them how they could be happy and prosperous once again. God had sent these missionaries to bring them this book. The chiefs were very pleased and asked the missionaries to return to them.

However, despite the *Bill of Rights* which grants all Americans the right to speech and religion, the U.S. Indian Agents said it was illegal for Americans citizens to enter the area without a permit. The missionaries were ordered to leave and were not permitted to return.

After a while, when the missionaries did not return, one of the chiefs traveled all the way to the head Indian Agency Office to ask for more information about the great book from heaven. The agents did their best to show the chief a good time, but they did not have anything that he wanted. When he learned that none of the men could help him, he said to the head agent:

I came to you over a trail of many moons from the setting sun. You were the friend of my fathers who have all gone the long way. I came with one eye partly opened, for more light for my people who sit in darkness. I go back with both eyes closed. How can I go back blind to my blind people? I made my way to you with strong arms, through many enemies and strange lands, that I might carry much back to them. I go back with both arms broken and empty... My people sent me to get the white man's Book from Heaven.

You took me where you allow your women to dance, as we do not ours, and the Book was not there. You took me where they worship the Great Spirit with candles, as we do not ours, the Book was not there. You showed me images of the Great Spirit and pictures of the good land beyond, but the Book was not among them. I am going back the long trail and sad trail to my people of the dark land.

You make my feet heavy with burden of gifts, and my moccasins will grow old in carrying them, but the Book is not among them. When I tell my poor people, after one more snow, the Council, that I did not bring the Book, no word will be spoken by our old men, and our young braves.

One by one they will rise and go out in silence. My people will die in darkness, and they will go on the long path to other hunting grounds. No white man will go with them, and no white man's book to make the way plain. I have no more words.

As disappointing as Oliver Cowdery's mission to the Indians turned out to be, both for the church and for our Lamanite brothers, the Lord did bless his missionaries with great success in the Ohio Valley and soon there were more members of the Church around the Kirtland area than in the whole state of New York. This was a blessing because enemies of the young restored church were starting to get bolder and the Prophet and the Saints needed to leave New York for safety.

Newel K. Whitney's Store where the Prophet Joseph Smith lived when he came to Kirtland, Ohio. This picture was taken by George Edward Andersen in 1907 while touring LDS Church History Sites.

Chapter Nine
Safety in the Wilderness
(December 9th)

Last time we talked about the organization of the Church in our day and how missionary work was beginning to enlarge our membership. In just a short time, the church grew from its original six members to over three hundred. Most of the new members lived in and around the small town of Kirtland, Ohio.

During the third General Conference of the Church in New York State, the Lord told the Saints that they were to sell their land in New York and move to Ohio. It was a powerful revelation. Today it is known as *Doctrine & Covenants*, section 38. You should read the whole section, but for now, here is an excerpt:

> Thus saith the Lord your God, even Jesus Christ, ... I show unto you a mystery, a thing which is had in secret chambers, to bring to pass even your destruction in process of time, and ye knew it not; But now I tell it unto you, and ye are blessed, not because of your iniquity, neither your hearts of unbelief; for verily some of you are guilty before me, but I will be merciful unto your weakness. Therefore, be ye strong from henceforth; fear not, for the kingdom is yours.
>
> And for your salvation I give unto you a commandment, for I have heard your prayers... I hold forth and deign to give unto you greater riches, even a land of promise, a land flowing with milk and honey, upon which there shall be no curse when the Lord cometh; And I will give it unto you for the land of your inheritance, if you seek it with all your hearts... I will be your king and watch over you. Wherefore, hear my voice and follow me, and you shall be a free people, and ye shall have no laws but my laws when I come, for I am your lawgiver, and what can stay my hand?... And again, I say unto you that the enemy in the secret chambers seeketh your lives. Ye hear of wars in far countries, and you say that there will soon be great wars in far countries, but ye know not the hearts of men in your own land... but if ye are prepared ye shall not fear... Wherefore, for this cause I gave unto you the commandment

that ye should go to the Ohio; and there I will give unto you my law; and there you shall be endowed with power from on high...

From this revelation the Saints learned many wonderful things. First of all, that the Lord was watching over them and was listening to their prayers. Second, that he knew of a plot to murder them. Thirdly, that he would give them a new home, a wonderful promised land where God alone would be their King. In order to obtain this blessing, He told the Saints that they needed to move to the Ohio Valley.

Many of the Saints were happy and believed that God was going to restore to them the long awaited land of Zion, but others were sad because they had nice homes and farms and didn't want to leave them.

The Prophet Joseph was eager to move to Ohio and to have all the members of the Church closer together. In January of 1831, he left New York for the American Frontier. A few weeks later, a sleigh containing several persons drove into Kirtland, Ohio right up to the doors of the mercantile store of Gilbert and Whitney. A stalwart young man sprang out, walked up the steps to the store where the junior partner was standing. Extending his hands as if to an old and familiar acquaintance, he exclaimed: "Newel K. Whitney, thou art the man." Mr. Whitney was astonished. He had never seen this person before.

"Stranger," Newel replied, "you have the advantage of me; I could not call you by name, as you have me."

"I am Joseph the Prophet," the young man said, smiling. "You've prayed me here, now what do you want of me?"

It was true. Just a short time prior to this, the Whitney family had prayed to God asking for direction in their lives. They invited the Prophet to live with them until he could find a place of his own.

I want you to listen carefully to this next story because it is about a young girl living in Kirtland who loved the *Book of Mormon* very much. Her name was Mary Lightner. Her uncle was Mr. Gilbert, Newel K. Whitney's partner in the mercantile store.

When Oliver Cowdery and the missionaries were going door to door in Kirtland preaching the gospel, quite a number of people joined the church including Mary and her mother.

Isaac Morley, a kind farmer in the area, was put in charge of the church. About this time, John Whitmer came and brought the first copy of the *Book of Mormon*. Mary remembered, "There was a meeting that evening, and we learned that Brother Morley had the book... the only one in that part of the country. I went to his house just before the meeting... and asked to see it.

Brother Morley put it in my hand. As I looked at it, I felt such a desire to read it, and I could not refrain from asking him to let me take it home and read it."

Since Brother Morley had not read it, he didn't want to let it go, but Mary pled so earnestly that he finally told her she could take the book if she promised to return it in the morning.

Mary said, "If any person in this world was ever perfectly happy in the possession of any coveted treasure, I was when I had permission to read that wonderful book."

Mary's family thought that it was very rude of Mary to borrow Brother Morley's book before he himself had a chance to read it. But, as the family members started taking turns with it, they got very excited. The next morning Mary got up early and read some more before keeping her promise to return it. When she reached Brother Morley's home, they were just waking up. She handed him the book.

"I guess you did not read much in it," he remarked.

Mary showed him how far she had read. Surprised, he said, "I don't believe you can tell me one word of it."

Mary then stood up straight and repeated from memory, "I, Nephi, having been born of goodly parents, therefore I was taught somewhat in all the learning of my father; and having seen many afflictions in the course of my days..." and so on. Then she gave him a general outline of the history of Nephi.

Brother Morley gazed at Mary in surprise, and said, "Child, take this book home and finish it, I can wait."

About the time Mary had finished the last chapter, the Prophet Joseph arrived in Kirtland. Mary continued, "Brother Whitney brought the Prophet Joseph to our house and introduced him to the older ones of the family. I was [outside] at the time." In looking around he saw the *Book of Mormon* on the shelf, "I sent that book to Brother Morley," he said surprised.

Mr. Gilbert told him how Mary had obtained it. He asked, "Where is your niece?" and Mary was sent for. She said, "When the Prophet saw me, he looked at me so earnestly, I almost felt afraid. After a moment or two he came and put his hands on my head and gave me a great blessing, the first I ever received. Then he made me a present of the book, and said he would give Brother Morley another."

Chapter Ten
Zion City
(December 10th)

The Prophet Joseph had not been in Kirtland long when the Lord gave him two important revelations. One was the location of the long awaited City of Zion and the other was a command to build a temple in Kirtland.

The plan for Zion City was different from anything seen on Earth before. It was to be a city laid out in a grid pattern in which each city block was ten acres square. In the center were three blocks reserved for church use. Two of the blocks were to contain 24 temples, two for each of the twelve tribes of Israel. The design was ingenious because in most frontier towns, families lived many miles apart. It was a very lonely life, especially for the women and children. The Lord's plan for Zion placed all the homes on half acre lots close together and the farms on the outskirts of town. This way children could attend school in town, woman could interact and work together and the men could enjoy the company of the community after work. The plan was also to stagger the houses in such a manner that no two homes had front doors facing each other. This gave the community more of a sense of privacy. Joseph thought this was wise since he worried that so many women living close together might waste their time gossiping about one another.

This wonderful city of Zion was to be the home of those who had clean hands and a pure heart. It can be a lot of work keeping your hands clean and purifying your heart, and some may not understand what this means. It is really very simple. Our heart is the source of our desires. When we want to do good things to help people, we have a kind and pure heart. When we hope that bad things happen to other people, or when we want to do something that is evil, that also comes from our heart. Our hands are how we do our work. If we hurt other people or steal from them, it is like having dirty hands, but if we use our hands to do good things and make the world a better place for God's children, it is like having clean hands. When Jesus returns to the Earth, he wants to live with people who do good things and have pure desires. We can be that people.

At the same time that Zion City was being planned in Missouri with its 24 temples, a single temple was being planned in Kirtland, Ohio. Now this may seem a little strange when you stop and think about it. Why would the Lord want the Saints to build 24 big temples in Zion City and still want a smaller temple to be built in Kirtland? It was for a very wise purpose. It is important that you never forget that while the Lord, his modern prophets, and the Saints are working hard to build up the Kingdom of God on the Earth, the devil is also busy trying to ruin everything. The devil knows that once the Kingdom of God is strong enough, his kingdom will be overthrown. The devil was determined to stop Zion City and her temples from being built. Unfortunately, the early Saints called upon to build the holy city were not righteous enough to stop him. However, the Lord knew all of this beforehand, and so, while Satan was busy trying to stop Zion from being built, the Lord was quietly building a temple in Kirtland. It is hard to fight a war on two fronts, even for Satan.

When Joseph and some of the brethren from Kirtland arrived at Independence, Missouri, it was a very backward place. A Christian missionary from another church had come to the area prior to the time the Saints arrived and described what he found there:

> [It was] such a godless place, filled with so many profane swearers... The majority of the people make a mild profession of Christian religion, but it is mere words... [The Sabbath day here] is a day of merchandising, jollity, drinking, gambling, and general anti-Christian conduct... There are a few so called ministers... hereabouts, but they are a sad lot of churchmen, untrained, uncouth, given to imbibing spirituous liquors, and indulging as participants, in the gambling... horse racing, and cock fighting...
>
> There are many suspicious characters who headquarter here, but when intelligence arrives that a federal marshal is approaching this county, there is a hurried scurrying of many... to the Indian territory...
>
> As soon as the marshal returns down stream, this element is back in the saloons and other centers of sin... There seems to be an over abundance of females practicing the world's oldest profession... Serious forms of violence are common... The sheriff has little support from the populace...

Such was the type of people that the god-fearing Mormons of Missouri moved among. Soon, there was going to be trouble. A short time after arriving, the Prophet Joseph took an ax and cut a path through the thick saplings until he found just the right spot. Then, he set up a stone and striped the bark from a section of a large nearby tree. He carved the letter T for temple on the tree's south side and the letters ZOM on the east side. The Prophet said that *Zomas* was an ancient term for Zion City. This was to be the spot for the first of Zion's Temples. During the dedication ceremony of the land, the Prophet read the 87th Psalm: "The Lord loveth the gates of Zion... Glorious things are spoken of thee, O city of God... And of Zion it shall be said, ... the highest himself shall establish her." God, Himself, would establish her. These words would later ring in the Saints' ears.

After Joseph set up the beginnings of Zion City he returned to Kirtland. While there were many persecutions both in

Missouri and in Ohio, there were many happy times as well, and many new members joined the church. One of these was Lorenzo Snow, who would later become the fifth president of the church. Lorenzo told of the first time he met the Prophet Joseph:

The first time I saw Joseph Smith, the Prophet of the Lord, I was seventeen years of age. It was rumored that he was going to hold a meeting in...Ohio, about four miles from my father's home... Having heard many stories about him, my curiosity was considerably aroused and I thought I would take advantage of this opportunity to see and hear him...

I made a critical examination as to his appearance, his dress, and his manner as I heard him speak. He was only twenty-five years of age and was not, at that time, what would be called a fluent speaker. His remarks were confined principally to his own experiences, especially the visitation of the angel, giving a strong and powerful testimony in regard to these marvelous manifestations. He simply bore his testimony to what the Lord had manifested to him, to the dispensation of the Gospel which had been committed to him, and to the authority that he possessed.

At first he seemed a little diffident and spoke in rather a low voice, but as he proceeded he became very strong and powerful, and seemed to affect the whole audience with the feeling that he was honest and sincere...

It was during these Kirtland years that many important revelations and commandments were given to the Church. Much of the happiness and good health that you enjoy today is because our Latter-Day Saint ancestors listened to the Lord and taught their children to obey His commandments. The most famous of these is the *Word of Wisdom*, now found in section 89 of the *Doctrine and Covenants*.

Like most revelation in the church, the Lord waits for us to ask Him what to do about a problem before giving us instruction. This is for a wise reason. The Lord is a God who loves freedom. He does not want to boss his people around and rule like a dictator. Instead, he teaches people how to live in happiness and waits for them to come to him for more instruction. That way he doesn't rob his children of their free agency. Free agency sounds like a confusing term until you know what it means. Free doesn't mean without cost. It means free as in freedom.

A free agent is a person who has the legal right to make up his own mind about something. Perhaps you have heard the term in sports. A baseball player who is a free agent can join whatever team he chooses. No one can sign a contract for a free agent; only that person can sign it. That is the way the Lord's kingdom works, every man and woman is a free agent to choose to join the Lord's kingdom or not.

The *Word of Wisdom* came about because the Prophet asked the Lord for more instruction about healthy living. It was during a time when the Prophet had started a school to teach the priesthood brethren more about the gospel. Brigham Young said this about the event:

The first School of the Prophets was held in a small room situated over the Prophet Joseph's kitchen, in a house which belonged to Bishop Whitney, and which was attached to his store...

Over this kitchen was situated the room in which the Prophet received revelations and in which he instructed the brethren. The brethren came to that place for hundreds of miles to attend school... When they assembled together in this room after breakfast, the first thing they did was to light their pipes and while smoking talk about the great things of the kingdom and spit [tobacco juice] all over the room; and as soon as the pipe was out of their mouths a large chew of tobacco would then be taken. Often when the Prophet entered the room to give the school instructions, he would find himself in a cloud of tobacco smoke. This, and the complaints of his wife in having to clean so filthy a floor made the Prophet think upon the matter, and he inquired of the Lord relative to the conduct of the elders in using tobacco, and the revelation known as the Word of Wisdom was the result of his inquiry.

The *Word of Wisdom* is one of the greatest gifts that God has given us in these last days to make us free from many of the diseases which causes so much suffering on Earth. The better the life we live, the better free agent we become. This also gives us more time to prepare to meet God. Something we all need.

Also, in those days before the *Word of Wisdom* was understood, all Christian churches used wine in their sacrament services. One Saturday night, early in the young Church's history, the Prophet Joseph saw that they had no wine for a Sunday Sacrament Meeting. He sent one of the brethren out to buy some wine, then went home for the evening to rest. As he walked along, suddenly an angel appeared to him with a warning. Some of the enemies of the church had a secret plan to poison the sacrament wine and kill all the Saints at once. This was very distressing since the Saints didn't know what to use for their sacrament.

Joseph asked the Lord what to do. He told the prophet to use water instead; that water was best because it was impossible to hide anything in pure water. The Lord then taught that it didn't matter that much what was used for the sacrament so long as the act was done in remembrance of Him and by the right authority (see D&C 27:1-5).

Chapter Eleven
Power from On High
(December 11th)

We have already talked about how wise the Lord was in preparing two temple locations at once and how difficult it was for Satan to stop the return of temples on the Earth. By saying that, I don't want you to think I mean that building the Kirtland Temple was easy. The Saints suffered many hardships to build our first temple. Sometimes people wonder why the Lord would have a poor and tired people work so hard to build a temple when many of them didn't have adequate means to take care of themselves.

It was because of a true principle. Have you ever heard the saying, "Where your heart is, there your treasure will be also?" Have you ever wanted something really bad and then worked hard to obtain it? How did it make you feel?

The Lord had a precious gift to give to the Saints, but he wanted them to really understand how important it was. They had to want it so much that they would give anything to obtain it. This gift was the Keys of God's Kingdom on Earth.

It is important to remember that Jesus Christ is a mighty King. Mighty kings have castles with beautiful audience halls in which to bestow gifts on their people. When it came time to give this wonderful gift to the people, our Heavenly King told Joseph Smith that he had no place to come to, or rather, "no place to lay His head."

The devil believed that the Lord would need to have the fantastic Zion City, with all its temples ready before he could give

His gifts of the Kingdom to the people. He was sure the Lord would want a temple like Solomon's or a city like Enoch's of old. But God was one step ahead of Satan and always has been from the beginning. He said, "I will not suffer that they shall destroy my work; yea I will show unto them that my wisdom is greater than the cunning of the devil."

When the Prophet Joseph told the Saints about the need to build a house for the Lord in Kirtland, they thought it was a great idea. Many suggested they build a large log cabin. Joseph was horrified, "Will you build a house unto the Lord of logs?!" He said that God needed a House as nice as they could build. But, who would build it? None of the Saints knew how to make a building as nice as a temple. It was then that Lorenzo Snow spoke up.

"I know a man who is capable of such construction," Lorenzo said.

"Who is he?" asked the Prophet.

"Artemus Millet," Lorenzo replied.

Artemus Millet was a wealthy and talented Canadian builder. The Prophet looked at Brigham Young and said, "I give you a mission to go to Canada and baptize Brother Artemus Millet and bring him to Kirtland. Tell him to bring a thousand dollars with him."

Brigham went to Canada and found Mr. Millet. When Artemus heard the Gospel he accepted it and left immediately for Kirtland to select the stone for the temple's foundation.

What further confused Satan was that this temple looked more like a big church house than any temple he had ever seen, but it was the Lord's design. Eliza Snow remembered the situation:

[When the Lord gave the command to build the Kirtland Temple] the Saints were few in number, and most of them very poor; and, had it not been for the assurance that God had spoken, and had commanded that a house should be built to his name, of which he not only revealed the form, but also designed the dimensions, an attempt towards building that Temple, under the then existing circumstances, would have been, by all concerned, pronounced preposterous.

The Saints were faithful anyway. They cut stone by day and guarded the construction site by night. The Prophet Joseph selected twenty-four priesthood holders to lay the corner-stones. Among those given this opportunity was a young man named Joseph Kingsbury. At the last minute the Prophet learned that Brother Kingsbury did not hold the Melchizedek Priesthood. Instead of dismissing him and giving his place to another, the Prophet took him aside and ordained him an elder. Brother Kingsbury remembered the Prophet's kindness in letting him participate for the rest of his life.

In order to help the poor of Kirtland, and those who gave their all to build the temple, the Prophet announced the beginning of Fast Day. At first it was on Thursdays. It was to be held once a month, as it is now, and all that would have been eaten that day: flour, meat, butter, fruit, or anything else, was to be carried to the fast meeting and put into the hands of the church to help take care of the poor.

When the Temple was finally finished there was a great manifestation of God's power. The brethren gathered together for its dedication. It could seat 960 but one thousand Saints crowded inside for the dedicatory service. Members of the church from every part of the country came together. The congregation was so large that many had to be turned away. They just kept packing them in until the building was full and they closed the doors.

One member, who had paid seven hundred dollars towards building the house, left the church because when he came late to the meeting, there was no more room and he was angry.

When the dedication prayer was read by Joseph, it was read from a printed copy. This was a great trial of faith to many. "How can it be that the prophet should read a prayer?" they said, "What an awful trial it was, for the Prophet to read a prayer!"

Despite some who did not have the right spirit about them, those who did attend with the right spirit saw amazing things. Frederick G. Williams saw the Savior. He came to the stand and accepted the dedication of the house. The Saints continued to experience many wonderful manifestations for several days.

Many individuals bore testimony that they saw angels. David Whitmer bore testimony that he saw three angels passing up the south aisle. Hundreds spoke in tongues, prophesying, or declaring visions.

Prescindia Huntington said, "I was in the temple with my sister. While the congregation was praying, we both heard, from one corner of the room above our heads, a choir of angels singing most beautifully. They were invisible to us, but myriads of angelic voices seemed to be united in singing a song of Zion, and their sweet harmony filled the temple of God."

The service of the dedication being over, it was repeated again on the next day, so that those who were unable to get in the first day could also attend.

On one particular Fast Day, Joseph's Father went to the temple very early before sunrise to pray and wait for the people to come. When he opened the meeting, he prayed fervently that the spirit of the Most High might be poured out as it was at Jerusalem, on the day of Pentecost—that it might come "like a mighty rushing wind." It was not long before it did come, to the astonishment of all. At first it so surprised Father Smith that he yelled out, "What! Is the house on fire?" But soon the congregation was filled abundantly with the spirit of revelation, prophecy and tongues as the Holy Ghost filled the whole house.

One week after the dedication services, on Easter Sunday, while all the Christian world was celebrating the resurrection of the Lord, and all the Jewish world was celebrating the Passover, Joseph Smith and Oliver Cowdery led the congregation in a worship service in the temple. After the afternoon session, the two men gathered near the Melchizedek Priesthood pulpits in the lower room of the temple and pulled the canvas veil. After they knelt in prayer, the veil of their minds parted and the Lord appeared, accepting the temple. Then, Moses appeared and restored the keys of gathering Israel and missionary work; Elias, the restorer, appeared and gave the keys of the gospel of Abraham; and finally, Elijah appeared with the keys of family history and temple work so that families could be sealed together both on Earth and in Heaven.

The Saints now had real power to build up the Kingdom. The Lord had been given a house in which to bestow His gifts to the Church, and He accepted their sacrifice in building it.

You will remember that we talked about the law of opposition. Well, a mighty gift had been given to the Saints, and so a period of trial and testing was coming.

An angry mob, made up of many so-called christians, tarred and feathered Joseph Smith one night. After the event, Joseph forgave the men and several later joined the church.

Chapter Twelve
Trouble in Zion
(December 12th)

You'll remember how we talked about the blessings and trials of the Saints in Kirtland, Ohio. We talked about how they overcame many hardships in order to build a temple where the Lord could bless them with power and keys to build His kingdom on Earth.

During this same time, the Saints in Missouri were having an equally difficult time building up the City of Zion. Many great names you will remember were there: Edward Partridge, W. W. Phelps, and others. They had built homes, shops, and a printing office. Many missionaries were going into the countryside and preaching the gospel and the good news that Zion City was going to be built in the state of Missouri. Many people joined the church and moved into the area. It was not long before some of the same lowlifes we spoke about earlier were very upset about what was happening. They accused the Saints of all kinds of bad behavior. It seemed that the Mormons could do nothing right.

Many historians are quick to blame the Mormons for causing the problems, but I for one don't believe that the Saints were as bad as the Missourians said they were. You have to remember that these Missourians were the same people who stole the Mormon's property, murdered and raped them. Evil people will do and say anything to get their way, even break the law and lie about it. While it is true that the Lord said the Saints were not righteous enough to establish the City of Zion, they were not so wicked as to deserve the treatment that Satan had in store for them. The Lord was very angry with the mobs of Missouri for the way they treated and lied about the Saints. Missouri paid a high price in later years, but that is a different story for another time. The real reason for all the trials the Saints suffered in Missouri was two-fold: they were not humble enough to establish Zion, and Satan was absolutely determined to stop them at any cost.

Because the Saints had a printing press in Missouri, it was decided that many of the Prophet's revelations should be compiled into a book so that more Saints could enjoy them. This was something that Satan could not allow. Do you remember young Mary Lightner who so loved the *Book of Mormon* that Joseph Smith gave her one as a present? She later moved to Independence and remembered these events:

A two story printing office was erected in Independence; altogether, the saints were in a prosperous condition, both temporally and spiritually in Missouri...

One evening the Brethren came to my uncle's house to converse upon the Revelations that had not been printed as yet, but few had looked upon them, for they were in large sheets, not folded. They spoke of them with such reverence, as coming from the Lord; they felt to rejoice that they were counted worthy to be the means of publishing them for the benefit of the whole world...

[As the time to bind Joseph's revelations into book form grew nearer, terrible threats were made] against our people, we were too much united to suit the inhabitants of Missouri, and they did not believe in our religion, or our way of doing business... We did not believe in slavery, and they feared us on that account, though we were counseled to have nothing to say to the slaves whatever, but to mind our own business.

Soon a mob began to collect in the town and set fire to the grain, and hay stacks in the yard of Bishop Partridge. All were destroyed. Then they began to stone the houses, breaking the doors and windows.

> One night, a great many got together and stoned our house... After breaking all the windows, they commenced to tear off the roof of the brick part amidst awful oaths and howls that were terrible to hear...

> The mob renewed their efforts again by tearing down the printing office, a two story building, and driving Brother Phelps's family out of the lower part of the house and putting their things in the street. They brought out some large sheets of paper, and said, "Here are the Mormon Commandments." My sister Caroline and myself were in a corner of a fence watching them; when they spoke of the commandments I was determined to have some of them. My sister said if I went to get any of them she would go too, but said "they will kill us."

> While their backs were turned, prying out the gavel end of the house, we went, and got our arms full, and were turning away, when some of the mob saw us and called on us to stop, but we ran as fast as we could. Two of them started after us. Seeing a gap in a fence, we entered into a large cornfield, laid the papers on the ground, and hid them with our persons. The corn was from five to six feet high, and very thick; they hunted around considerable, and came very near us but did not find us.

Another hero of the day was Elder John Taylor who would later become the third president of the church. When John Taylor learned of the intended raid, he asked Bishop Partridge if he could go and secure some copies of the scriptures. Bishop Partridge told him the mob would surely kill him if he was discovered. John replied that he would risk his life to have a few copies. Bishop Partridge told him he could try.

John Taylor, a young man at the time, watched as the mob tried to burn Joseph's revelations. He saw that some of the pages of the *Book of Commandments* were thrown into an old log stable. He said:

> I ran my hands into a crack between the logs, and pulled out a few of the printed sheets at a time until I got as many as I could carry.

> When I was discovered, a dozen men surrounded me and commenced throwing stones at me, and I shouted out, "Oh My God must I be stoned to death like Stephen for the sake of the word of the Lord?" The Lord gave me strength and skill to elude them and make my escape without being hit by a

stone. I delivered the copies to Bishop Partridge, who said that I had done a good work and my escape was a miracle.

Soon these outrageous crimes exploded into all out war. When the Prophet heard that Bishop Partridge and Brother Allan had been tarred and feathered, and put into prison; that some of the brethren had been tied to trees and whipped until the blood ran down their bodies; that some had been killed and others shot, the Prophet was overwhelmed by the news. His response shows the nature of his soul. He did not fume with rage or become hateful and bitter. Upon hearing this, the Prophet burst into tears and said through his sobs, "Oh my brethren! My brethren! Would that I had been with you, to have shared your fate."

A church council was called and it was resolved to form an armed militia, called the *Camp of Zion*, to bring relief to the suffering Saints. During the meeting the point was raised that the Kirtland Saints had no money in which to prepare a militia.

Joseph Smith said, "Brethren, don't get discouraged about our not having means. The Lord will provide and he will put it into the heart of somebody to send me money."

The very next day Joseph received a letter from Sister Vose, containing one hundred and fifty dollars. When he opened the letter, he took out the money and held it up, exclaiming, "See here, did I not tell you the Lord would send me some money to help us on our journey? Here it is."

Chapter Thirteen
Zion's Camp
(December 13th)

On the fifth of May, 1834, the Prophet and nearly 100 men started to march from Kirtland to Missouri. By the end of the journey they would march about nine hundred miles in just three weeks. Their mission was to protect the saints in Missouri and encourage the governor there to restore the Saints' property, which was taken illegally by the mobs. By the end of the journey, the militia would grow into 204 men. The Prophet organized them into companies of 12 men each. Ahead of the group, a man marched with a white flag bearing the word PEACE in red letters.

As they passed through the State of Indiana, they had to cross some very bad swamps. They had to attach ropes to the wagons to pull them through. Joseph was always first in line pulling on the rope in his bare feet.

By the time the camp crossed the Wakandaw River, they had traveled twenty-five miles without resting or eating. They were very tired and found a nice place to camp. When the Prophet reached the camp site, he said that they must travel further on. Taking the lead, he invited the brethren to follow him another seven miles to a Mormon township called *Allred Settlement* where the Allred Brothers: James, Isaac, William and John lived.

This caused a split in the camp. Lyman Wight and others refused to follow the Prophet; they were tired and wanted to stay put. Finally, after some convincing, they followed him. It was a very good thing they did because it turned out that a mob was hiding nearby with orders to attack the camp once they were asleep.

Many interesting and miraculous stories took place during the march of Zion's Camp. One day they came upon a thick woods. Suddenly the Prophet felt very depressed and told the brethren that there had been a great deal of bloodshed in that place. He remarked that, "Whenever a man of God is in a place where many have been killed, he will feel lonesome and unpleasant, and his spirit will sink."

About forty rods from where the Prophet made this observation they came upon a farm. On their left, was a mound sixty feet high that occupied about a acre of land. All around it, apple trees grew in a neat and cultivated pattern. When the brethren approached the mound they found that it had holes dug in it disclosing human bones. Hyrum said he believed that a great army had been slain and piled up there. He commented that it was customary for ancient peoples to bury large numbers of men above the ground by piling dirt upon them. Since many of the battles of the Jaredites and the final battles of the Nephites took place in North America, it seemed to the men of the camp as evidence of the *Book of Mormon*.

Later the camp would pass a mound built on a bluff about 300 feet high. The Prophet would later write:

During our travels we visited several of the mounds which had been thrown up by the ancient inhabitants of this country, Nephites, Lamanites, etc., and this morning I went up on a high mound, near the river, accompanied by the brethren. From this mound we could overlook the tops of the trees and view the prairie on each side of the river as far as our vision could extend, and the scenery was truly delightful.

On the top of the mound were stones which presented the appearance of three altars having been erected one above the other, according to the

ancient order; and the remains of bones were strewn over the surface of the ground. The brethren procured a shovel and a hoe, and removing the earth to the depth of about one foot, discovered the skeleton of a man, almost entire, and between his ribs the stone point of a Lamanite's arrow, which evidently produced his death...

I discovered that the person whose skeleton was before us was a white Lamanite, a large, thick-set man, and a man of God. His name was Zelph. He was a warrior and chieftain under the great prophet Onandagus, who was known from the Hill Cumorah to the Rocky mountains. The curse was taken from Zelph... one of his thigh bones was broken by a stone flung from a sling, while in battle, years before his death. He was killed in battle by the arrow found among his ribs, during the last great struggle of the Lamanites and Nephites.

It is very sad that many people today think that all *Book of Mormon* history took place in Mexico or North America. Joseph Smith certainly didn't believe this. He clearly taught that the people lived from South America to Canada. He once told the Saints that the Narrow Neck of Land mentioned in the *Book of Mormon* was the Isthmus of Panama.[1]

If there was one lesson the Lord wanted the Elders of Zion's Camp to learn, it was to trust Him and have faith in the living Prophet. There are so many stories about this. One day some of the brethren found a large quantity of turtle eggs in a sand bar. They were very excited about them since their meals had been scanty. They were about to cook them up when Joseph warned them, "Those are not turtle eggs but snake eggs. You must not eat them."

But some of the men said they knew the difference between turtle eggs and snake eggs. Plus they added, a Prophet doesn't have any say over things like eggs. Joseph warned them again, "Eat snakes' eggs, will you? The man that eats them will be sorry for it; you will be sick." Despite Joseph's warning, several of the men ate them and were violently sick for a whole day.

On another occasion, the men of Zion's Camp stopped at the town of Atlas where a local man offered them some hams in exchange for work. Since there was not enough ham for the entire camp, the Prophet's company decided to go without. Instead of ham they ate mush and honey which hardly satisfied them but they wanted their brethren to eat well.

The Prophet had just finished his scanty meal when several of the men threw their ham at the door of the Prophet's tent saying, "We won't eat dirty, stinking meat."

The Prophet called the cook and told him to quickly fry up the ham for his company as they had sacrificed for others during the past 48 hours and were very hungry. The cook immediately fried the ham for the Prophet's company and they ate until they were completely satisfied. They claimed that they had never tasted better ham in their life.

Many of the brethren were faithful, but many were not. Those that were not, grumbled, and refused to trust in the Lord's mighty power. Toward the end of their march, the Camp stopped to repair their wagons between the forks of the Fishing River near the towns of Richmond and Liberty, Missouri. Seeing that the Mormons were trapped by the steep banks of the River, a mob of three hundred took advantage of the situation. Five men, representing the mob, rode into the camp and swore to kill the Prophet and all the Mormons. Heber C. Kimball recorded what happened next:

Soon after these men left us we discovered a small black cloud rising in the west, and not more than twenty minutes passed away before it began to rain and hail...

All around us the hail was heavy; some of the hailstones, or rather lumps of ice, were as large as hens' eggs. The thunders rolled with awful majesty, and the red lightnings flashed through the horizon, making it so light that I could see to pick up a pin almost any time throughout the night.

The earth quaked and trembled, and there being no cessation it seemed as though the Almighty had issued forth His mandate of vengeance. The wind was so terrible that many of our tents were blown down. We were not able to hold them up; but there being an old meeting house close at hand, many of us fled there to secure ourselves from the storm...

The mob came to the river two miles from us, but the river had risen [forty feet and] they were obliged to stop without crossing over. The hail fell so heavily upon them that it beat holes in their hats, and in some instances even broke the stocks off their guns; the horses, being frightened, fled, leaving the riders on the ground. Their powder was wet, and it was evident that the Almighty fought in our defense.

The next day the camp arrived at Liberty, Missouri but the Prophet decided not to enter the city. The Prophet told both the camp members and the officers from Missouri, that their purpose was only to assist the persecuted Saints. He had no intention of injuring any of the Missourians nor starting a war. The officers were satisfied with the statement but several of the brethren were not. They claimed they would rather die than return home without a battle. Joseph told them that due to their disobedience and lack of humility before God a number of the camp would, "die like sheep with the rot" and that there was nothing he could do to help them.

When the sheriff arrived, Joseph proposed that both the Saints and the officials of Missouri choose six men to decide the course of action for the suffering saints. However, the Lord had another idea. He revealed His will to the Prophet in what is now section 105 of the *Doctrine and Covenants*. The Lord was not pleased with this plan and the grumbling warlike attitude of many of the men in Zion's Camp. Zion was not going to be built and argued over by a committee, and it was not going to be a city of blood. The Lord reminded the Saints, "For behold, I do not require at their hands to fight the battles of Zion; for, as I said in a former commandment, even so will I fulfill — I will fight your battles." We must remember this, Zion is the Lord's and He will fight for her. It is not our job to negotiate Zion's needs.

A few days later a severe outbreak of cholera hit the camp. Joseph and Hyrum tried to administer to the suffering men, but as Joseph said, "I quickly learned by painful experience, that when the great Jehovah decrees destruction upon any people, and makes known His determination, man must not attempt to stay His hand." As a punishment for trying to intervene, Joseph and Hyrum found themselves immediately seized with cholera themselves. They prayed for God to spare them from the awful pain. Hyrum said:

> ...the disease immediately fastened itself upon us and in a few minutes we were in awful agony. We...fell upon our knees and cried unto the Lord that he would deliver us from this awful calamity, but we arose worse than before. We kneeled down the second time, and when we commenced praying the cramp seized us, gathering the cords in our arms and legs in bunches and operating equally severe throughout our system. We still besought the Lord, with all our strength, to have mercy upon us, but all in vain. It seemed as though the heavens were sealed against us, and that every power that could render us any assistance was shut within its gates. [Joseph and I] then kneeled down the third time, concluding never to rise to our feet again until one or the other should get a testimony that we should be healed; and that the one who should get the first intimation of the same from the Spirit, should make it known to the other.

After praying some time the cramp began to release its hold. In a short time, Hyrum sprang to his feet and exclaimed, "Joseph, we shall return to our families. I have had an open vision in which I saw our mother kneeling under an apple tree; and she is even now asking God, in tears, to spare our lives, that she may again behold us in the flesh. The Spirit testifies that her prayers, united with ours, will be answered."

"Oh, my mother!" Joseph said, "how often have your prayers been the means of assisting us when the shadows of death encompassed us."

The attack lasted four days. In the end, it left sixty-eight sick and fourteen dead. The cholera that started in the Camp soon spread over the whole country. As the men marched back home they saw all the various towns affected with it. It continued to spread eastward and according to Edson Barney was the source of the Great Cholera Epidemic of 1834.

Although many criticized the Prophet for the apparent failure of Zion's Camp, the Lord, however, said it best: "it is expedient in me that they should be brought thus far for a trial of their faith."

Wilford Woodruff had this to say about the experience:

When the members of Zion's Camp were called, many of us had never beheld each others' faces; we were strangers to each other and many had never seen the prophet. We had been scattered abroad, like corn sifted in a sieve, throughout the nation. We were young men, and were called upon in that early day to go up and redeem Zion, and what we had to do we had to do by faith... We accomplished a great deal, though apostates and unbelievers many times asked the question, "What have you done?"

We gained an experience that we never could have gained in any other way. We had the privilege of beholding the face of the prophet, and we had the privilege of traveling a thousand miles with him, and seeing the workings of the Spirit of God with him, and the revelations of Jesus Christ unto him and the fulfillment of those revelations. And he gathered some two hundred Elders from throughout the nation in that early day and sent us broadcast into the world to preach the Gospel of Jesus Christ.

Had I not gone up with Zion's Camp I should not have been here today, and I presume that would have been the case with many other [men] in this Territory. By going there we were thrust into the vineyard to preach the Gospel, and the Lord accepted our labors.

Later the Lord would decree that the first Twelve Apostles of the last dispensation were to be selected from the faithful men of Zion's Camp. This was a very great honor and reward.

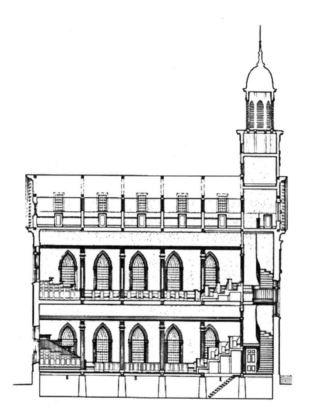

Architectural drawing of the Kirtland Temple showing its interior layout. Today the Kirtland Temple is in the care of the *Community of Christ* church who gives tours and watches after the building.

Chapter Fourteen
Glimpses of Kirtland
(December 14th)

We have had several difficult stories to wade through, but although these were difficult times, there were happy times as well. Here are a few of my favorite stories from Kirtland.

You have heard of the *Pearl of Great Price*. It is one of the Holy Scriptures of our people. One of the sections in the *Pearl of Great Price* is the *Book of Abraham*. Here is the miraculous story of how it came to be.

While Joseph had been laboring in Kirtland, journeying to and from Missouri, teaching his brethren and being taught of God, the Lord was sending the Saints a gift from one of the catacombs of the Pharaohs; the writings of Father Abraham and Father Joseph, governor of Egypt.

On the 7th day of June, 1831, a French explorer discovered, at great expense, an Egyptian tomb containing several hundred mummies. Of these, only eleven were moveable. He carried them away, but died on his return voyage to Paris. In his will, the mummies were given to his nephew, Michael H. Chandler of America.

Hoping to discover some treasure of precious stones or metals, Mr. Chandler opened the coffins. Attached to two of the bodies were rolls of linen preserved with the same care and apparently by the same method as the bodies. Within the linen coverings were rolls of papyrus perfectly preserved. The learned men of Philadelphia flocked to see them. Mr. Chandler asked many scholars to interpret some of the characters. Even the wisest among them were only able to guess at the meaning of a few of the signs.

Mr. Chandler heard that a Prophet lived in Kirtland who could decipher strange languages. As he traveled west showing them, he finally reached Kirtland and presented himself to Joseph with four of the mummies and the rolls of manuscript.

The Prophet, under inspiration of the Almighty, interpreted some of the ancient writings to Mr. Chandler's satisfaction. He was pleased to see that Joseph's interpretation was similar to the learned men of Philadelphia, but Joseph's insight was so much deeper.

Later, some of the friends of the Prophet purchased the mummies with the writings and Joseph began to interpret the rolls and strips of papyrus. The result of his labor was to restore to the world the *Book of Abraham*. The Prophet further went on to say that the other scroll contained the writings of Joseph who had been sold into Egypt. Unfortunately, the Prophet's time was not such that he could restore this important book to the church.

Another informative story from the Kirtland days of the Church comes from the memory of William Cahoon. While still a young man, Brother Cahoon was called to be the Prophet's home teacher.:

I was called and ordained to act as a teacher to visit the families of the Saints. I got along very well till I found that I was obliged to call and pay a visit to the Prophet. Being young, only about seventeen years of age, I felt my weakness in visiting the Prophet and his family in the capacity of a teacher. I almost felt like shrinking from duty. Finally I went to his door and knocked, and in a minute the Prophet came to the door. I stood there trembling, and said to him:

"Brother Joseph, I have come to visit you in the capacity of a [home] teacher, if it is convenient for you."

He said, "Brother William, come right in, I am glad to see you; sit down in that chair there and I will go and call my family in."

They soon came in and took seats. He then said, "Brother William, I submit myself and family into your hands," and then took his seat. "Now Brother William," he continued "ask all the questions you feel like."

By this time all my fears and trembling had ceased, and I said, "Brother Joseph, are you trying to live your religion?"

He answered "Yes."

I then said "Do you pray in your family?"

He said "Yes."

"Do you teach your family the principles of the gospel?"

He replied "Yes, I am trying to do it."

"Do you ask a blessing on your food?"

He answered "Yes."

"Are you trying to live in peace and harmony with all your family?"

He said that he was.

I then turned to Sister Emma, his wife, and said "Sister Emma, are you trying to live your religion? Do you teach your children to obey their parents? Do you try to teach them to pray?"

To all these questions she answered "Yes, I am trying to do so."

I then turned to Joseph and said, "I am now through with my questions as a teacher; and now if you have any instructions to give, I shall be happy to receive them."

He said "God bless you, Brother William; and if you are humble and faithful, you shall have power to settle all difficulties that may come before you in the capacity of a teacher."

I then left my parting blessing upon him and his family, as a teacher, and took my departure.

In the Lord's kingdom even the Prophet Joseph Smith had a home teacher and when he called upon the family, the Prophet was never too busy to let him in.

On one occasion in a meeting with the Twelve Apostles, the Prophet Joseph pledged that he would not speak a word until all of the twelve had first spoken their mind on a matter of interest to the general body. He remained quiet for nearly 18 hours. After they all had spoken, Joseph said, "You have caught me this once and I now want to give you some advice. Never get caught as I have. Never go into a corner unless you can see your way out in some manner." The Prophet was a man so true to his word that he would rather remain silent for a whole day due to a quick and foolish pledge than break his word. However, once all the brethren had spoken he used his own mistake to educate them on not making hasty vows or promises.

Here is one more wonderful story. During the School of the Prophets in Kirtland, Brother Zebedee Coltrin witnessed an amazing event which should bring great comfort to every member of the church; proof of the Father and the Son's concern and watchful presence over the Saints:

I believe I am the only living man now in the church who was connected with the School of the Prophets when it was organized in 1833, the year before we went up in Zion's Camp...

Every time we were called together to attend to any business, we came together in the morning about sunrise, fasting and partook of the Sacrament each time; and before going to school we washed ourselves and put on clean linen.

At one of these meetings... when we were all together, Joseph having given instructions, and while engaged in silent prayer, kneeling, with hands uplifted each one praying in silence, no one whispered above his breath, a personage walked through the room from East to West, and Joseph asked if we saw him.

I saw him and supposed the others did, and Joseph answered, "that is Jesus, the Son of God, our elder brother." Afterward Joseph told us to resume our former position in prayer, which we did. Another person came through; He was surrounded as with a flame of fire.

For a moment Brother Coltrin feared that the entire building would burst into flames due to the beings unspeakable consuming fire of great brightness. The Prophet Joseph said, "That was God the Father."

Brother Coltrin described him as "surrounded as with a flame of fire, which was so brilliant that I could not discover anything else but His person. I saw His hands, His legs, His feet, His eyes, nose, mouth, head and body in the shape and form of a perfect man... [His] appearance was so grand and overwhelming that it seemed I should melt down in His presence and the sensation was so powerful that it thrilled through my whole system and I felt it in the marrow of my bones."

The Lord has said many times that he is in our midst but that we can not see him.

Well, as you can read in many accounts, the banking laws of the United States changed about this time to allow for independent organizations to run banks and print their own money. The Saints chose to open a bank of their own, but due to the greed of a few, it proved to be a disaster. As you might expect, many blamed Joseph for the trouble. As the spirit of apostasy overtook Kirtland, the Lord sent Heber C. Kimball on a mission to England to bring some new blood into the church.

In the end, Joseph had to flee from Kirtland for his life, but once again the wisdom of the Lord was greater than the devil's secret plans. Even though the City of Zion had not materialized in Missouri, the prophet had gained the Keys of the Kingdom in

Kirtland and the Saints in Missouri were ready and able to receive him.

It is said that things got so bad in Kirtland that some of the Prophet's former friends planned to murder him. At the last minute, he was warned of the plot and hidden in a cupboard, which was placed on an ox cart and driven out of town. Once out of danger, he was given his favorite horse, Old Charley, on which he rode to the safety of the Saints in Missouri.

Chapter Fifteen
The Central Place
(December 15th)

We have already talked about Zion City but there is still more to say. You will remember from your Bible Studies that the first man was named Adam and that his wife, our first mother, was named Eve. After our Father in Heaven made their bodies, he placed them on this Earth in a beautiful garden called the Garden of Eden. Here flowers and fruit trees grew up everywhere and there were no weeds or grass to mow. It was a paradise.

Do you know the story of how God told our first parents that everything in the garden belonged to them? They could eat any fruit they wanted except one. It was called the forbidden fruit and it grew on a tree called the Tree of the Knowledge of Good and Evil. Do you remember that Satan tricked Eve into eating the fruit? Then poor Adam had to eat it also since he loved Eve too much to leave her all alone. Well, what is important to know is this; the Garden of Eden you read about in the *Bible* was located at Independence, Missouri at the very place where our people wanted to build Zion City! A church scholar, B. H. Roberts knew all about this place. He said:

> The soil is a rich [and black], in places... Both climate and soil are favorable to the production of all the fruits and vegetables of the warm temperate climate... also apples, pears, apricots, persimmons, plums of many varieties, the luscious peach, the delicious grape, and a great many kinds of berries...
>
> [There are trees such as] hickory, some black walnut, a variety of oaks, plenty of elm, cherry, honey locust, mulberry, basswood, and box elder, huge sycamore and cottonwood in the river bottoms, also hard and soft maple.

Formerly many wild animals roamed over the prairies, or lived in the woods, such as the buffalo, elk, deer, bear, wolf, beaver, and many smaller animals, together with wild turkeys, geese, quail, and a variety of singing birds... it was once the hunter's paradise...

Such is the land of Zion... a land of surpassing loveliness, though its beauties are marred rather than increased by those who inhabit it.

You can see why the Saints loved this place so much. Do you remember from your Bibles that after Adam and Eve ate the forbidden fruit, they had to leave? Well, they moved to a new home in the valley of Adam-ondi-Ahman. It was there that God taught Adam how to sacrifice on an altar. It was there that Cain killed Abel. It was a valley a few miles north of Independence. When Joseph Smith moved some of the Saints up to Adam-ondi-Ahman and told them all about this place, I am sure some thought this story was too fantastic. Most people believe all these events happened in the Middle East, but we know better.

One day, while the Prophet was at Adam-ondi-Ahman, he gathered some men together, "Get me a spade and I will show you the altar that Adam offered sacrifice on," he said. One of the men in attendance, Chapman Duncan, witnessed what happened. "We went forty rods north of my house. [Joseph] placed the spade with care, placed his foot on it. When he took out the shovel full of dirt, it bared the stone. The dirt was two inches deep on the stone I reckon. About four feet or more was disclosed. He did not dig to the bottom of the layers of good masonry... The stone looked more like dressed stone, nice joints, ten inches thick, eighteen inches long or more."

This was Father Adam's altar. Heber C. Kimball also saw it:

[Joseph] led us a short distance to a place where there were ruins of three altars built of stone, one above the other, the one standing a little back of the other, like unto the pulpits in the Kirtland Temple... "There," said Joseph, "is the place where Adam offered up sacrifice after he was cast out of the garden." The Altar stood at the highest point of the bluff. I went and examined the place several times while I remained there.

There were other altars around the area, including an ancient Nephite altar which further proves that the *Book of Mormon* peoples enjoyed the whole of the land of North and South America during their history. Unfortunately today, Adam's Altar has disappeared. In about 1922, it is reported that a man, going by the name of Joe Miller, had the stones packed up and shipped away.

One of my personal favorite stories from Missouri comes from the memory of Bishop Edward Partridge. One day while the Prophet was at Bishop Partridge's house in Far West, Missouri, he was asked about the Lost Ten Tribes. The Prophet stated that they were hid from us by land and air. Bishop Partridge assuming that Joseph had made a mistake said, "You mean they are hidden by land and water."

"No", said the Prophet, "By land and air. They are hid from us in such a manner and at such an angle that the astronomers cannot get their telescopes to bear on them from this earth." The Prophet spoke a lot about the time when the Lost Ten Tribes would return bearing their scriptures and genealogies. He said that their return would add great strength to the church.

As the mobs became more and more nasty to the Saints, a battle became inevitable. Have you heard of the terrible murders at Haun's Mill? Some have said, since Joseph was a prophet, why didn't he foresee this terrible massacre and stop it? Here are the facts:

Brother Haun owned a grist mill in a small Mormon community. As the mobs were increasing their violence toward the Saints, the citizens of this little town called a meeting. They appointed Brother Haun to go to the Prophet for advice on what to do about the violence.

"Move into the city," was the Prophet's prompt reply.

"What!" Brother Haun declared, "and leave the mill?"

"Yes, leave the mill."

"To the mob?"

"Yes, to the mob."

"But," responded the selfish mill-owner, "Brother Joseph, we think we are strong enough to defend the mill and keep it in our own hands."

"Oh, well," replied the Prophet, "if you think you are strong enough to hold the mill, you can do as you think best."

What more could the Prophet say? His method had always been to give his counsel when asked for and let people make up their own mind. He would never take away another man's right to be a free agent.

Brother Haun returned and reported that Brother Joseph's counsel was for them to stay and protect the mill. Which of course, was something he didn't say. The Saints did stay and after a terrible battle, almost all of them were killed.

Chapter Sixteen
Brother Smith Goes to Washington
(December 16th)

The Kirtland and Missouri Era was a difficult time for our people. During the last two readings we learned that many Saints in Kirtland apostatized. In Missouri, the mobs became so bloodthirsty that our people had to abandon their homes and leave Zion to the mobs.

In order to get some justice, the Lord instructed the Saints to write up their stories and appeal their case to the highest levels of earthly power. After no local and state authorities would help them, the Prophet went to Washington D.C., right up to Congress and the President of the United States.

The trip was a long one. Our Prophet had to travel through the mountains between Philadelphia and the capital by stagecoach. At a rest stop, the driver left his passengers for a moment. While he was gone, the horses became frightened and ran. As the couch raced faster and faster, the passengers were terrified. Joseph, however, was cool and brave.

He calmed his fellow travelers and even stopped one hysterical woman from throwing her baby out of the window. Then, he opened the door and, securing a hold on the side the coach, pulled himself up by sheer strength to the driver's seat. Gathering up the reins, he gained control of the horses and slowed the coach to a stop.

The passengers felt they owed Joseph their lives and praised him for his bravery. Some of the passengers, who were members of Congress, said they would speak of the brave deed on the floor of the Congress. Then, they asked their rescuer his name. When he said Joseph Smith the Mormon, all their gratitude and praise ceased at once and nothing more was said about it during the trip nor in Washington D.C.

During this time in our nation's history, the President of the United States was Martin Van Buren. You will find Van Buren severely criticized by some; but when we think what a hard position he had to fill just after Andrew Jackson's hot-headed career, we shall wonder that he did as well as he did.

Van Buren was unlike Andrew Jackson in many ways. Jackson believed that the President of the United States had to be a strong leader, telling Congress what to do and vetoing any bills that went too far. Van Buren thought a President should work quietly, making sure that any laws Congress wanted to pass were enforced.

Van Buren was a very good natured man but didn't like to take a stand on anything. He always tried to see every side of a problem and tried to make everybody happy, and so he usually made nobody happy. Here is an example. One time a senator accepted a bet that he could make President Van Buren take a stand on something. He said to the President, "It's been rumored that the sun rises in the east. Do you believe it?"

"Well," Van Buren replied, "I understand that's the common acceptance, but as I never get up till after dawn, I can't really say."

President Van Buren may have thought that his approach was the best way to run a country but it allowed two very terrible things to happen. Perhaps you have heard of them. The first is called "The Extermination Order" and the second, "The Trail of Tears."

We are only going to talk about, "The Extermination Order," but "The Trail of Tears," which happened to our Lamanite brothers and sisters, was very sad indeed. In order to understand how awful "The Extermination Order" was, you have to know something about the American Bill of Rights.

You will remember that our Bill of Rights sets out in law certain freedoms that our foundering fathers said no government had the right to take away from the people. Rights like the ability to own private guns; the right to speak out against injustices, and the right to worship God anyway we please. We who grew up having these freedoms, don't understand how very precious they are. In the days before the American Revolution, some of our colonies had a law that men and women had to belong to a certain church or worship God in a certain way that the government thought was best. There had been many wars and many deaths in the old world over this belief. You will remember how in some of our colonies a man could be arrested if he missed too many church meetings. This is because there was no separation between church and state. In our Bill of Rights it says, "Congress shall make no law respecting the establishment of religion or prohibiting the free exercise thereof."

Many people are confused about what separation of church and state means; they think that our Constitution says that churches and religious philosophies have no place in government, but that, of course, is silly. What our Constitution actually says is that government cannot make any law telling churches and people who they must worship or which church they must belong to. It also says that the government cannot make people give money to or support any church nor can the government establish a church or control a church. And so it is that something very sad happened to the Mormons in Missouri.

Our people have always been hard workers and soon they were prosperous and happy in Missouri. We have already read about how backward and cruel the Missourians could be.

When it came time for the next election, the mob wouldn't let our people vote. Now, every American citizen has the right to vote, and the Mormons were American citizens. Anyway, when the Mormons got mad, the mobs went straight to the Governor of Missouri, Lilburn W. Boggs, and made up stories about what the Mormons had done. Some of the old settlers who had watched all of the trouble which the mobs were stirring up, and knew that the Mormons were innocent, went to the Governor with the truth. But, the Governor coldly replied, "The quarrel is between the Mormons and the mob, and they can fight it out."

When the mob leaders saw that the governor wouldn't stop them, they got really bold. They burned down Mormon houses, shot little boys and men, stole cows and pigs and did many terrible things. They even imprisoned Joseph Smith in a cold, dark dungeon called the Liberty Jail. As things got worse, the Governor decided that the Mormons had to go. He issued "The Extermination Order."

Extermination seems like a heavy word and surely it is because it means, "to get rid of by killing." Today we call this kind of thing genocide. Perhaps you have heard how Adolf

Hitler ordered the extermination of Jews and how awful that was. Well, right here in the United States, citizens with rights, whose fathers and mothers had fought for "life, liberty and the pursuit of happiness" in the Revolutionary War were denied any rights and ordered to leave their homes or be exterminated!

The Saints did leave. They left Adam-ondi-Ahman, Adam's Altar, Tower Hill, and their hopes and dreams for Zion City. The Saints figured they had lost about one and a half million dollars in goods and property. That was a lot of money in 1840. It was for this reason that Joseph Smith went to meet with President Van Buren and took with him all the stories the Saints had written about their loses.

When President Van Buren read these histories, he looked at our Prophet and said, "Your cause is just, but I can do nothing for you. If I take up with you I shall lose the vote of Missouri." That was a very cowardly thing to say, but we have already seen how President Van Buren refused to take a stand on anything. And, by the way, he was not re-elected to the Presidency anyway.

Joseph Smith riding one of his favorite mounts, Black Charlie, in a parade with the *Nauvoo Legion*. The Prophet loved the *Nauvoo Legion* as it was proof to him, and all the Saints, of their Constitutional Freedoms of religion and the right to bear arms for personal and civil protection.

Chapter Seventeen
The City Beautiful
(December 17th)

The terrible trials the Saints suffered in Missouri did not go unnoticed by the citizens of the State of Illinois. They welcomed our people to their State. Many of the Saints found friendship in and around the town of Quincy.

Brigham Young led the exodus from Missouri to Illinois since our Prophet was still imprisoned in Liberty Jail at the time. It was good practice for Brother Brigham, and he would later say that this experience helped him better organize the Saints' exodus into the Salt Lake Valley years later. Once Joseph was able to get out of Missouri, he joined his family in Quincy. The Prophet was only in Illinois a short time when he made plans to build a new city for the Saints. He choose a large swampy farm with a few buildings on it along the Mississippi River. It was known as Commerce, Illinois, but the Prophet renamed it Nauvoo, an ancient Hebrew word meaning Beautiful Place. It was a prophetic and hopeful name for a dirty old swamp, but it was the best the poor Saints could do. They knew that in time the Lord would bless it. Here is the story of how Nauvoo started.

When Joseph Smith first came to Commerce, a Mr. White, was living there. He offered to sell the Prophet his farm for $2,500 with $500 up front and the rest one year later. Joseph and the brethren were talking about this offer when some of them said: "We can't buy it, for we lack the money."

Joseph took out his purse and, emptying out its contents, gave each of the brethren a half dollar, leaving him penniless.

Addressing the brethren he said: "Now you all have money and I have none: but the time will come when I will have money and you will have none." He then told Bishop Knight: "You go back and buy that farm!"

Bishop Knight went to White, but learned that he had raised the price one hundred dollars since the first meeting. The Bishop returned to Joseph without closing the bargain. Joseph again sent him with orders to purchase the farm, but Bishop Knight, finding that White had raised the price still another hundred dollars, returned again without purchasing it.

For the third time Joseph commanded him to go and buy the farm and ordered him not to come back till he had done so. When Bishop Knight got back to White, he had raised the price again making the whole amount $2,800! However, the bargain was closed and the contract drawn up; but how the money was going to be raised neither Bishop Knight nor the other brethren could see.

The next morning Joseph and several of the brethren went down to Mr. White's to sign the contract and make the first payment on the land. A table was brought out with the papers upon it and Joseph signed them. Then he moved back from the table and sat with his head down as if in thought for a moment. Just then a man drove up in a carriage and asked if Mr. Smith was there. Joseph hearing his name, got up and went to the door.

The man said, "Good morning, Mr. Smith, I am on a speculation today, I want to buy some land and thought I would come and see you." Joseph pointed around to all the land that he had just signed the contract for, but the man said: "I can't go with you today to see the land. Do you want any money this morning?"

Joseph replied that he would like some and when the stranger asked, "How much?" the Prophet told him "Five hundred dollars."

The man walked into the house with Joseph, emptied a small sack of gold on the table and counted out that amount. He then handed to Joseph another hundred dollars, saying: "Mr. Smith, I make you a present of this!"

After this transpired, Joseph laughed and said to the brethren: "You trusted in money; but I trusted in God. Now I have the money, and you have none."

The Saints got busy draining the swampy land around Nauvoo but it was not soon enough, for disease attacked our people. Wilford Woodruff witnessed much of the sickness at the time, and he also witnessed the power of the priesthood to heal:

While I was living in a cabin in the old barracks of Commerce, we experienced a day of God's power with the Prophet Joseph. It was a very sickly time and Joseph had given up his home in Commerce to the sick. He had a tent pitched in his yard and was living in that himself. The large number of Saints who had been driven out of Missouri, were flocking into Commerce; but had no homes to go into. They were living in wagons, in tents, and on the ground. Many, therefore, were sick through the exposure they were subjected to. Brother Joseph had waited on the sick, until he was worn out and nearly sick himself.

On the morning of the 22nd of July, 1839, he arose, reflecting upon the situation of the Saints of God in their persecutions and afflictions. He called upon the Lord in prayer, and the power of God rested upon him mightily, and as Jesus healed all the sick around Him in His day, so Joseph, the Prophet of God, healed all around him on this occasion. He healed all in his house, then in company with Sidney Rigdon and several of the Twelve, he went among the sick lying on the bank of the river and he commanded them in a loud voice, in the name of Jesus Christ, to come up and be made whole. They were all healed. When he healed all that were sick on the east side of the river, they crossed the Mississippi river in a ferry-boat to the west side, to Montrose, where we were.

The first house they went into was President Brigham Young's. He was sick on his bed at the time. The Prophet went into his house and healed him, and they all came out together. As they were passing by my door, Brother

Joseph said: "Brother Woodruff, follow me." These were the only words spoken by any of the company from the time they left Brother Brigham's house till we crossed the public square, and entered Brother Fordham's house. Brother Fordham had been dying for an hour, and we expected each minute would be his last.

When we entered the House, Brother Joseph walked up to Brother Fordham, and took him by the right hand; in his left hand he held his hat.

He saw that Brother Fordham's eyes were glazed, and that he was speechless and unconscious.

After taking hold of his hand, he looked down into the dying man's face and said: "Brother Fordham, do you not know me?" At first he made no reply; but we could all see the effect of the Spirit of God resting upon him.

He again said: "Elijah, do you not know me?"

With a low whisper, Brother Fordham answered, "Yes!"

The Prophet then said, "Have you not faith to be healed?"

The answer, which was a little plainer than before, was: "I am afraid it is too late. If you had come sooner, I think I might have been."

He had the appearance of a man waking from sleep. It was the sleep of death. Joseph then said: "Do you believe that Jesus is the Christ?"

"I do, Brother Joseph," was the response.

Then the Prophet of God spoke with a loud voice, as in the majesty of the Godhead: "Elijah, I command you, in the name of Jesus of Nazareth, to arise and be made whole!"

The words of the Prophet were not like the words of man, but like the voice of God. It seemed to me that the house shook from its foundation.

Elijah Fordham leaped from his bed like a man raised from the dead. A healthy color came to his face, and life was manifested in every act... It was the greatest day for the manifestation of the power of God through the gift of healing since the organization of the Church.

In a very short time, a beautiful city began to rise along the banks of the Mississippi River. While it was not the Zion City the Saints had wanted, it was a beautiful place of rest to re-gather and wait until the Lord made his will known again to the church.

Chapter Eighteen
A Prophet and a Brother
(December 18ᵗʰ)

In Nauvoo, the greatness of Joseph Smith was realized and the Saints and the world got an opportunity to see the man of God up close. From Nauvoo, the Prophet would shake the foundations of Earth and Hell. He would tutor men, like Brigham Young and Heber C. Kimball, who would later settle half a continent. He would expound the mysteries of God and free the human mind to understand them.

The short segment of life remembered as Nauvoo would show Joseph as Militiaman, Statesman, Mayor, Philosopher, Translator, Revelator, Educator, Civil Architect, Scientist, Scriptorian, Author, Theorist, and Brother Joseph, Prophet of God, to the Saints who loved him. Here are a series of stories to illustrate the kind of man our Prophet was:

> One day the Prophet promised a sister in the church that she would receive a witness to the truthfulness of his teachings if she would earnestly pray for it. This sister found a quiet place out between three haystacks and knelt down to pray. She raised her arms to heaven and prayed her most sincere prayer for the Lord to give her the heavenly witness that Joseph had promised.
>
> A few nights later when she was in the same bed as her aunt, an angel appeared to her. He was spectacular to look at with eyes like flashing lightning. Suddenly she became afraid and shook her aunt hoping to awaken her. She shut her eyes tightly as her aunt awoke just in time to see the angel depart.
>
> The next Sunday Joseph asked her if she had received her witness yet. The sister replied, "No".
>
> The Prophet shook his head and told her that was strange since he was expressly told that she would.

"I have not had a witness," the woman corrected, "but I have seen something I have never seen before. I saw an angel, and I was frightened almost to death."

The Prophet put his face in his hands, "How could you be such a coward?" he said.

"I was weak," she returned.

"Did you think to say, Father, help me?" the Prophet asked.

"No," she said.

"Well, if you had just said 'Father, help me,' your mouth would have been opened. That was the Angel of the Living God. He came to you with more knowledge, intelligence and light than I ever dared to reveal."

The Prophet told her not to worry for she would still see greater things than that if she remained faithful.

One day, after a certain brother in the church had noticed the Prophet working very hard around his yard, decided to give him some advice. He told the Prophet, "Brother Joseph, my wife does much more hard work than your wife does." He went on to say that the Prophet ought to let his wife take more of the load, as some of the work the Prophet was doing was beneath his position.

Brother Joseph looked at the man kindly and said, "If a man cannot learn in this life to appreciate his wife and do his duty by her in properly taking care of her, he need not expect to have her in the hereafter."

The Brother later said humbly, "His words shut my mouth as tight as a clam. I took them as a terrible reproof." After that he tried to do better by the good wife he had and tried to lighten her burdens and help her more with his manly strength.

One day a Sister in the church went to the Prophet's house to make an accusation against one of the brethren for saying something scandalous about her. When her complaint had been heard, the Prophet asked her if she was quite sure that what the brother had said about her was utterly untrue. She was quite sure that it was. He then told her to think no more about it, for it could not harm her. If untrue, it could not live, but the truth would survive.

Still she felt that she should have some redress. Then he offered her his method of dealing with such cases for himself. When an enemy had told a scandalous story about him, which had often been done, before he rendered judgment he paused and let his mind run back to the time and place of the setting of the story to see if he had not by some unguarded word or act laid the block on which the story was built. If he found that he had done so, he then forgave his enemy, and felt thankful that he had received a warning of a weakness which he had not known he possessed.

Then he said to the sister that he would have her do the same. Search her memory thoroughly and see if she had not herself unconsciously laid the foundation for the scandal that annoyed her.

She thought deeply for a few moments and then confessed that she believed she had. Then the Prophet told her that in her heart she could forgive that brother who had risked his own good name and her friendship to give her a clearer view of herself. The sister thanked her advisor and went away in peace.

One day a group of boys and girls were playing "Anthony-Over," usually shortened to "anti-i-over," in which two teams of children on opposite sides of a house, having one ball, throw it over the roof. The team on the other side waits for its arrival and if anyone catches it, the entire team then tries to get to the other side of the house without being tagged by the opposite team. Not having a soft rubber ball, they were using a hard wooden one, and not having permission, they were using an old man's house. Well the racket of that wooden ball crashing on the old man's roof was quite a shock to him. He ordered the children to go away.

Joseph Smith passed by and saw the discouraged look on the children's faces.

"Let's walk over to the carpenter shop," he said. There Joseph picked scraps of wood from the waste box and asked the carpenter to make some tippies for the children on his foot-powered lathe.

While the carpenter was doing that, Joseph secured more scraps and asked the children to whittle paddles to strike the tippies. Then he took them to Main Street, the widest street in town, and showed them how to strike the tippy with the edge of the paddle. When it flew upward, he showed them how to bat the airborne tippy with the paddle toward a distant goal.

The Prophet set the goal for the rock quarry at the head of Main Street. The children then played with the tippies, trying to whack them toward the goal each time they came to rest on the ground. The children said it gave them good exercise, tested their muscular skills, and kept them from breaking up an old man's roof.

One morning when a group of newly baptized Mormons were arriving for the first time in Nauvoo, the Prophet dressed up in rough-looking clothes, got on his horse and rode to where the new converts were preparing to enter the city.

He stopped Brother Rushton and asked in a rough-sounding voice, "Are you a Mormon?"

"Yes sir," he replied.

"What do you know about old Joe Smith?" the Prophet asked.

"I know that Joseph Smith is a prophet of God."

"I suppose you are looking for an old man with a long, gray beard. What would you think if I told you I was Joseph Smith?"

"If you are Joseph Smith, I know you are a prophet of God," he returned.

"I am Joseph Smith," the Prophet said, this time in his regular voice. "I came to meet you, dressed as I am in rough clothes and speaking in this manner, to see if your faith was strong enough to stand the things that are coming. If not, you should turn back right now." Of course, none of them did turn back.

And my very favorite story: One day in Nauvoo two boys were having a fistfight in front of the hotel on Main Street. The City Council was in session on the second floor of Joseph Smith's Red Brick Store. The Prophet Joseph, then mayor of Nauvoo, was presiding at the meeting. Looking through the window toward the Northeast, he saw the two boys fighting. Turning the meeting over to one of the aldermen to conduct, he ran down the stairs, across the street, vaulted over a fence, and reached the boys just as they had pulled pickets from a fence and were about to beat each other with them.

Joseph grabbed each boy by his shirt collar and ordered them to throw down their weapons. Then, releasing his grip on them asked, "Don't you know that no one in this town is allowed to fight except me?"

Sheepishly the boys admitted they hadn't known that. Then the Prophet said, "Next time you feel like fighting someone come to my home and ask for a fight and I'll fight you, and it will be legal."

The boys quickly ended their fight and made up. It was well known that the Prophet was the best wrestler in town and could easily beat anyone in a fair fight, if he wanted to. One of the boys told the other, "I surely don't want to fight Brother Joseph!"

"Neither do I," said the other.

Chapter Nineteen
A Man of God
(December 19th)

As we approach the Prophet's birthday, it is proper that we spend a little time listening to the words he taught the Saints. We will begin with an excerpt from Joseph's famous "Essay on Happiness."

> Happiness is the object and design of our existence; and will be the end thereof, if we pursue the path that leads to it; and this path is virtue, uprightness, faithfulness, holiness, and keeping all the commandments of God. But we cannot keep all the commandments without first knowing them, and we cannot expect to know all, or more than we now know unless we comply with or keep those we have already received. That which is wrong under one circumstance, may be, and often is, right under another.
>
> God said, "Thou shalt not kill;" at another time He said "Thou shalt utterly destroy." This is the principle on which the government of heaven is conducted—by revelation adapted to the circumstances in which the children of the kingdom are placed. Whatever God requires is right, no matter what it is, although we may not see the reason thereof till long after the events transpire. If we seek first the kingdom of God, all good things will be added. So with Solomon: first he asked wisdom, and God gave it him, and with it every desire of his heart, even things which might be considered abominable to all who understand the order of heaven only in part, but which in reality were right because God gave and sanctioned by special revelation.
>
> A parent may whip a child, and justly, too, because he stole an apple; whereas if the child had asked for the apple, and the parent had given it, the child would have eaten it with a better appetite; there would have been no stripes; all the pleasure of the apple would have been secured, all the misery of stealing lost.
>
> This principle will justly apply to all of God's dealings with His children. Everything that God gives us is lawful and right... He never will institute an ordinance or give a commandment to His people that is not calculated in its nature to promote that happiness which He has designed, and which will not end in the greatest amount of good and glory to those who become the

recipients of his law and ordinances. Blessings offered, but rejected, are no longer blessings, but become like the talent hid in the earth by the wicked and slothful servant...

Our heavenly Father is more liberal in His views, and boundless in His mercies and blessings, than we are ready to believe or receive; and, at the same time, is more terrible to the workers of iniquity, more awful in the executions of His punishments, and more ready to detect every false way, than we are apt to suppose Him to be. He will be inquired of by His children. He says: "Ask and ye shall receive, seek and ye shall find;" but, if you will take that which is not your own, or which I have not given you, you shall be rewarded according to your deeds; but no good thing will I withhold from them who walk uprightly before me, and do my will in all things—who will listen to my voice and to the voice of my servant whom I have sent; for I delight in those who seek diligently to know my precepts, and abide by the law of my kingdom; for all things shall be made known unto them in mine own due time, and in the end they shall have joy.

Here are a few more sayings of the Prophet Joseph:

"I shall speak with authority of the Priesthood in the name of the Lord God... If you wish to go where God is, you must be like God, or possess the principles which God possesses, for if we are not drawing towards God in principle, we are going from Him and drawing towards the devil. Yes, I am standing in the midst of all kinds of people.

Search your hearts, and see if you are like God. I have searched mine, and feel to repent of all my sins.

We have thieves among us, adulterers, liars, hypocrites. If God should speak from heaven, he would command you not to steal, not to commit adultery, not to covet, nor deceive, but be faithful over a few things. As far as we degenerate from God, we descend to the devil and lose knowledge, and without knowledge we cannot be saved, and while our hearts are filled with evil, and we are studying evil, there is no room in our hearts for good, or studying good. Is not God good? Then you be good; if He is faithful, then you be faithful. Add to your faith virtue, to virtue knowledge, and seek for every good thing.

The Church must be cleansed, and I proclaim against all iniquity. A man is saved no faster than he gets knowledge, for if he does not get knowledge, he will be brought into captivity by some evil power in the other world, as evil spirits will have more knowledge, and consequently more power than many men who are on the earth. Hence it needs revelation to assist us, and give us knowledge of the things of God."

We get a glimpse into Joseph's inner-world when he told the Saints:

It is my meditation all the day, and more than my meat and drink, to know how I shall make the Saints of God comprehend the visions that roll like an overflowing surge before my mind. Oh! how I would delight to bring before you things which you never thought of! But poverty and the cares of the world prevent. But I am glad I have the privilege of communicating to you some things which, if grasped closely, will be a help to you when earthquakes bellow, the clouds gather, the lightnings flash, and the storms are ready to burst upon you like peals of thunder. Lay hold of these things and let not your knees or joints tremble, nor your hearts faint; and then what can earthquakes, wars and tornadoes do? Nothing.

Here are a few more interesting things the Prophet taught the Saints:

The devil cannot read the thoughts in your head, but the moment you speak he knows your mind; he can hear, and if you do not tell your plans the devil can not lay plans to counteract yours.

Never be discouraged. If I were sunk in the lowest pit of Nova Scotia, with the Rocky Mountains piled on me, I would hang on, exercise faith, and keep up good courage, and I would come out on top.

Children are the honor, glory, and royal diadem of womanhood.

The Lost Ten Tribes are not on this globe, but a portion of this earth had cleaved off with them and when the time comes when the "earth reels to and fro like a drunken man and the stars from heaven fall," it will be them joining us again.

If any man is hungry, let him come to me, and I will feed him at my table. If any are hungry or naked, come and tell me, and I will divide with them to the last morsel; and then if they are not satisfied, I will kick them in their backside.

From my boyhood up to the present time I have been hunted like a tender deer upon the mountains. I have never been allowed to live like other men. I have been driven, chased, stoned, whipped, robbed, mobbed, imprisoned, persecuted, accused falsely of everything bad. I have suffered till the Lord knows I have suffered enough.

The Lord once told me that I could have whatever I asked Him for in His name. I have been afraid to ask God to kill my enemies, because some of them might still repent and be saved.

Whenever you commence something new, you have to enter a horn [either by the wide open bell side or the tight, little pipe]. Always go in at the little end of the horn; for if you do not, but enter at the big end, you will have to either turn round and come out again or go out through the tighter small end and be squeezed to death.

I want to speak about lawyers. I have good feelings towards them; nevertheless I will reprove the lawyers and doctors anyhow. Jesus did, and every prophet has too; and if I am a prophet, I shall do it too. Our lawyers have read so little that they are ignorant. Don't employ lawyers, or pay them money for their knowledge, for I have learned that they don't know anything. I know more than they all. When I am going to study law, this is the way I study it: I fall asleep and the Almighty God teaches me the principle of law.

Many ministers hate me and cry out asking: "Why is it that this babbler gets so many followers and can keep them?" I answer: "It is because I possess the principle of love. All that I offer the world is a good heart and a good hand."

And lastly, a very important one for us today:

I will give you a key that will never rust — if you will stay with the majority of the Twelve Apostles, and the records of the Church, you will never be led astray.

Chapter Twenty
The King Follett Sermon
(December 20th)

On Sunday, April 7th, 1844, a few months before our prophet was murdered by a mob, he was asked to speak at the funeral of a man named King Follett. The sermon that he gave has become known as the *King Follett Discourse*. It is one of the most important sermons the Prophet ever gave because it separated members of our Church from the rest of secular-christianity forever. Every other Christian church on earth believes that God the Father, Jesus Christ and the Holy Ghost are a mysterious spiritual power that is completely incomprehensible to the human mind. Maybe you have heard some people say that God has no body and that he is so big that he can be everywhere at the same time, and yet he is so small that he can fit right inside your heart. Or, that the Father and the Son somehow share one body between them. Joseph Smith knew this was not true. He had seen the Father and the Son in the First Vision and knew that they were glorious men, each with his own human body.

In the *King Follett Sermon*, Joseph revealed a mystery that had never been known on earth before. It was a mystery that would later guarantee his death. Even today members of secular christian churches say that Joseph Smith taught many good things and that they could agree with Joseph if only he had not said the *Book of Mormon* was true and only if he had not given us the *King Follett Discourse*. It is important that every member of our Church read the entire sermon but for now, here is an excerpt:

Beloved Saints... I want your prayers and faith that I may have the instruction of Almighty God and the gift of the Holy Ghost, so that I may set

forth things that are true and which can be easily comprehended by you, and that the testimony may carry conviction to your hearts and minds of the truth of what I shall say...

In the first place, I wish to go back to the beginning—to the morn of creation. There is the starting point for us to look to, in order to understand and be fully acquainted with the mind, purposes and decrees of the Great Elohim, [our Heavenly Father] who sits in yonder heavens as he did at the creation of the world...

There are but a very few beings in the world who understand rightly the character of God. The great majority of mankind do not comprehend anything, either that which is past, or that which is to come, as it respects their relationship to God. They do not know, neither do they understand the nature of that relationship; and consequently they know but little above the brute beast, or more than to eat, drink and sleep. This is all man knows about God or His existence, unless it is given by the inspiration of the Almighty...

I want to ask... every man, woman and child, to answer the question in their own hearts, what kind of a being God is?... I will prove that the world is wrong, by showing what God is. I am going to inquire after God; for I want you all to know Him, and to be familiar with Him; and if I am bringing you to a knowledge of Him, all persecutions against me ought to cease. You will then know that I am His servant; for I speak as one having authority...

God himself was once as we are now, and is an exalted man, and sits enthroned in yonder heavens! That is the great secret. If the veil were rent today, and the great God who holds this world in its orbit, and who upholds all worlds and all things by His power, was to make himself visible,—I say, if you were to see him today, you would see him like a man in form like yourselves in all the person, image, and very form as a man; for Adam was created in the very fashion, image and likeness of God, and received instruction from, and walked, talked and conversed with Him, as one man talks and communes with another... We have imagined and supposed that God was God from all eternity. I will refute that idea, and take away the veil, so that you may see.

These are incomprehensible ideas to some, but they are simple. It is the first principle of the gospel to know for a certainty the character of God, and to know that we may converse with Him as one man converses with another, and that He was once a man like us; yea, that God himself, the Father of us all, dwelt on an earth, the same as Jesus Christ Himself did; and I will show it from the Bible.

I wish I was in a suitable place to tell it, and that I had the trump of an archangel, so that I could tell the story in such a manner that persecution would cease forever. What did Jesus say? The scriptures inform us that Jesus said, as the Father hath power in himself, even so hath the Son power— to do what? Why, what the Father did. The answer is obvious—in a manner to lay down his body and take it up again. Jesus, what are you going to do? To lay down my life as my Father did, and take it up again. Do you believe it? If you do not believe it you do not believe the Bible. The scriptures say it, and I defy all the learning and wisdom and all the combined powers of earth and hell together to refute it. Here, then, is eternal life—to know the only wise and true God; and you have got to learn how to be gods yourselves, and to be kings and priests to God, the same as all gods have done before you, namely, by going from one small degree to another, and from a small capacity to a great one; from grace to grace, from exaltation to exaltation, until you attain to the resurrection of the dead, and are able to dwell in everlasting burnings, and to sit in glory, as do those who sit enthroned in everlasting power. And I want you to know that God, in the last days, while certain individuals are proclaiming His name, is not trifling with you or me... To inherit the same power, the same glory and the same exaltation, until you arrive at the station of a god, and ascend the throne of eternal power, the same as those who have gone before. What did Jesus do? Why, I do the things I saw my Father do when worlds came rolling into existence. My Father worked out His kingdom with fear and trembling, and I must do the same; and when I get my kingdom, I shall present it to My Father, so that He may obtain kingdom upon kingdom, and it will exalt Him in glory. He will then take a higher exaltation, and I will take His place, and thereby become exalted myself. So that Jesus treads in the tracks of His Father, and inherits what God did before; and God is thus glorified and exalted in the salvation and exaltation of all His children. It is plain beyond disputation, and you thus learn some of the first principles of the gospel, about which so much hath been said.

When you climb up a ladder, you must begin at the bottom, and ascend step by step, until you arrive at the top; and so it is with the principles of the gospel—you must begin with the first, and go on until you learn all the principles of exaltation. But it will be a great while after you have passed through the veil before you will have learned them. It is not all to be comprehended in this world; it will be a great work to learn our salvation and exaltation even beyond the grave. I suppose I am not allowed to go into an investigation of anything that is not contained in the Bible. If I do, I think there are so many over-wise men here that they would cry "treason" and put me to death. So I will go to the old Bible and turn commentator today...

I will transpose and simplify [the Bible's original Hebrew into] the English language... In the beginning, the head of the Gods called a council of the Gods; and they came together and [prepared] a plan to create the world and people it. When we begin to learn this way, we begin to learn the only true God, and what kind of a being we have got to worship. Having a knowledge of God, we begin to know how to approach Him, and how to ask so as to receive an answer.

When we understand the character of God, and know how to come to him, he begins to unfold the heavens to us, and to tell us all about it. When we are ready to come to him, he is ready to come to us. All sins shall be forgiven, except the sin against the Holy Ghost; for Jesus will save all except the sons of perdition.

I advise all of you to be careful what you do, or you may by-and-by find out that you have been deceived. Stay yourselves; do not give way; don't make any hasty moves, you may be saved. If a spirit of bitterness is in you, don't be in haste. You may say, that man is a sinner. Well, if he repents, he shall be forgiven. Be cautious: wait. When you find a spirit that wants bloodshed,—murder, the same is not of God, but is of the devil. Out of the abundance of the heart of man the mouth speaketh.

The best men bring forth the best works. The man who tells you words of life is the man who can save you. I warn you against all evil characters who sin against the Holy Ghost; for there is no redemption for them in this world nor in the world to come.

I could go back and trace every object of interest concerning the relationship of man to God, if I had time. I can enter into the mysteries; I can enter largely into the eternal worlds...

Rejoice, O Israel! Your friends who have been murdered for the truth's sake in the persecutions shall triumph gloriously in the celestial world, while their murderers shall welter for ages in torment, even until they shall have paid the uttermost farthing. I say this for the benefit of strangers.

I have a father, brothers, children, and friends who have gone to a world of spirits. They are only absent for a moment. They are in the spirit, and we shall soon meet again. The time will soon arrive when the trumpet shall sound. When we depart, we shall hail our mothers, fathers, friends, and all whom we love, who have fallen asleep in Jesus. There will be no fear of mobs, persecutions, or malicious lawsuits and arrests; but it will be an eternity of felicity...

Hear it, all ye ends of the earth—all ye priests, all ye sinners, and all men. Repent! Repent! Obey the gospel. Turn to God; for your religion won't save you, and you will be damned. I do not say how long...

I have intended my remarks for all, both rich and poor, bond and free, great and small. I have no enmity against any man. I love you all; but I hate some of your deeds. I am your best friend, and if persons miss their mark it is their own fault. If I reprove a man, and he hates me, he is a fool; for I love all men, especially these my brethren and sisters...

I cannot lie down until all my work is finished. I never think any evil, nor do anything to the harm of my fellow-man. When I am called by the trump of the archangel and weighed in the balance, you will all know me then. I add no more. God bless you all. Amen.

It is said that Joseph later told some friends that because he had dared to give the world the *King Follett Discourse*, Satan would kill him.

Joseph Smith preaching to the American Indians. Joseph Smith loved the native peoples of America. He taught that they were part of the Lost Tribes of Israel and needed to be treated with kindness. Our *Book of Mormon* is a book about them and how much God still loves them. It was Joseph's example that lead later Mormon leaders to teach our people, "Befriend the Indians. They are our Brothers. Feed them, don't fight them." Many years later the U.S. Government would teach evolution; a racist doctrine that says that Indians and *all colored peoples* are less-human than other lighter-skinned peoples. That is not true. The *Book of Mormon* proves that all men are brothers, equally important to God. It says that our Indian brothers are Israelites and the children of Father Lehi who was a great man and prophet.

Chapter Twenty One
Brother Joseph
(*December 21st*)

While at Nauvoo, the Prophet was still not free of the mobs from Missouri. They felt that he had illegally escaped punishment from their State, and they wanted him back. On one occasion, John Bellows was having a conversation in the Prophet's home when two officers from Missouri arrived to force the Prophet illegally back to their State:

[One morning] we went down to Joseph's Mansion to have an interview with the Prophet. We found him at home. He met us at the door smiling. At the same time he put out his hand and shook hands with my father first, and then grasped my hand, at the same time inviting us to come in. I cannot describe the feelings I had when he grasped my hand. I thought he was the best and noblest man my eyes ever beheld. He led us into the sitting room, where we conversed for over an hour. Joseph and my father did most of the talking: now and then he would ask me a few questions, and paid considerable attention to me.

While we were in the Prophet's house a knock was heard at the door. Joseph opened the door, and there stood two well-dressed men with tall, black stove-pipe hats. One of the men asked if Mr. Smith was in. Joseph said, "Yes, sir, I am the man."

There was silence for a moment, and then Joseph spoke up and said, "Gentlemen, I know what is in your hearts, but you do not know what is in mine; and I know who you are. You are officers from Missouri to arrest me. Wait a minute," he said, "till I get my hat and I will go with you."

He turned around and made a polite bow and said, "Brother Bellows, please excuse me; call in again."

At this, father and I followed Joseph out of the door. Joseph and the officers took the lead, and father and I went on behind until we reached the gate. Here Joseph grasped the two men, one with each arm. This aroused my curiosity. I wanted to see the end, so I followed behind. Joseph led them to where some men were at work on the Nauvoo House. He led them around, and showing them the different rooms explained to them the design of the building. Presently they went inside, out of my sight. I stayed there a short time and then returned to my stopping place. I had not been there more than thirty or forty minutes when the news was all over town that the officers from Missouri had come for Joseph and that they could not find him. How he got away from the officers I never learned. [It seemed that the Prophet just disappeared.]

On one occasion, Joseph was invited to visit a tribe of Indians in Iowa and give them some advice. An Indian agent stated that he would act as interpreter between Joseph and the Tribe. Hoping to anger the Indians, the interpreter did not tell the Indians what Joseph was actually saying. Instead he told them that the Mormons were going to destroy them with a large army.

The Indians listened to this false interpretation until they began to grunt and move about nervously. Soon they were picking up stones or pieces of wood to use as weapons to kill the white man's prophet who dared to come into their homes with a message of death for their people.

In a miraculous manner, Joseph Smith understood every word his deceitful interpreter was saying. He stepped forward with as much bravery as any warrior in the audience ever manifested, pushed aside the falsifying interpreter, and began to speak to the men in their own tongue. The moment his voice was heard, a calm spirit of understanding settled upon the warriors. They dropped their weapons. Joseph's speech was long and eloquent. Every word of which fell upon the ears of his hearers as if he had spent his whole life in their villages, learning their speech as well as they themselves knew it.

This was a miracle to the natives. They knew that the pale face prophet-chief was a true son of the Great Spirit. When the results of this meeting were told to other tribes, they too began to visit Nauvoo seeking advice from the Great Pale Faced Prophet.

Once while the Prophet was preaching at an outdoor Sabbath meeting, several little boys were sitting on the steps of the platform on which the Prophet Joseph Smith stood. Policemen came by and ordered the boys off the steps, but the Prophet turned to them and said, "Let the boys alone; they may hear something that they will never forget." How the little children loved his kindness towards them and when they were adults and fathers told their own children about it.

All the little children loved the Prophet, the little girls thought he was so handsome and the little boys wanted him to play on their baseball teams.

One little girl wanted to go to church with her aunt because she heard that the Prophet would be speaking in that congregation. She begged to be allowed to sit on the end of the bench where she could get a better view of the Prophet as he came in. She was so excited that she could hardly wait to see him. As he walked up the aisle, she stretched out her tiny hand and touched his cloak.

The next day she felt the center of attention as she played with the other young girls. "The Prophet's cloak touched my hand," she said, holding it out for the other children to admire. "See! I held it out like this. It was this right hand here!" All the other girls were jealous that she got to touch the Prophet.

Louisa Roundy remembered that each child felt proud to help protect the Prophet. They would willingly play their part, which was no small one, in throwing his enemies off his track when they sought to entrap him. The smallest boy on the streets of Nauvoo could not be tricked into telling anything concerning the Prophet's whereabouts. Each had an evasive answer ready for any questioner he encountered.

Once when Louisa was ten or eleven, she was playing with a group of children in the street. A stranger rode up to them and offered money to any child who would tell him where he could find "Old Joe Smith."

One little boy piped up, "Why, he just rode by, on a white horse on his way into heaven." After a few more futile attempts to bribe the children, the stranger gave up in disgust, and rode angrily away from the Prophet's loyal little friends.

As a child, Adeline Hatch remembered a time when she was visiting the Prophet's children at their home. The Prophet was walking up and down their long hall wrapped in deepest thought. The little girl had heard people say that this was the way he communed with the Lord, so she was interested in watching him.

Two of his sons were engaged in a merry bit of fun. They were walking up and down the hall after their father, trying to take long steps like he did. Whenever one of the boys took such a big step that he nearly overbalanced, there was much noisy laughter from the children on the sidelines. Besides this, both boys were wearing new shoes that squeaked loudly. Altogether there was a good deal of racket. The Prophet was quite unperturbed. So great was his power of concentration, whenever he was engaged in thinking, that he was not even aware of conditions which most people would have found very disturbing. He never said a harsh word to his children while they were playing joyfully.

The Prophet had great love for his family and his wife Emma. Once while William W. Phelps was dining with the Prophet, Emma entered the room and served up dinner.

"What a kind, provident wife I have," said Joseph, "when I want a little bread and milk, she loads the table with good things to destroy my appetite!"

"You should do as Bonaparte did," Phelps suggested, "have a table just large enough for the victuals you want yourself."

Whereupon Emma remarked, "Mr. Smith is bigger than Bonaparte; he can never eat without his friends."

The Prophet was deeply touched by the remark and told Emma that he had never been paid a nicer compliment by anyone. A kind word from his wife gave him all the confidence he needed when things seemed hard.

On the afternoon that the Prophet died, animals throughout the city of Nauvoo acted very strangely. Cattle bellowed, roosters would not stop crowing and city dogs hallowed repeatedly in the streets. The Saints also felt a terrible sadness come over them. Soon afterwards, the news spread through the city that Joseph and Hyrum Smith had been murdered. It was a very sad time for our people.

Chapter Twenty Two
A Prophet Martyred
(December 22nd)

We have talked a lot about how Missouri believed that Joseph Smith had illegally escaped their clutches and wanted him back to stand trial. The truth of the matter was simple. Their plan had been to imprison the prophet in Liberty Jail throughout the winter — even though they knew he was innocent — hoping he would die of exposure. If he did happen to survive the bitter cold, their next plan was to simply delay his trial forever until he died in prison. Now, every American citizen has the right to a speedy and fair trail, but the Missourians knew they had no real case against the Prophet. They needed a way to kill him and make it look like an accident.

When Joseph was permitted to escape from Missouri into Illinois, through the kindness of some local sheriffs who understood the plot, the Missourians were really angry. They were determined to kill him. You have already heard about one attempt to kidnap the Prophet and how he mysteriously disappeared. There are many stories such as these.

As long as the Prophet stayed in the State of Illinois, he was legally safe from Missouri. That only made his enemies more angry. Missouri demanded that Illinois turn Joseph over to them, but the people of Illinois remembered how cruel the Missourians had been to the Mormons, and so, for a time, the Prophet was safe. Things did become so ugly, however, that the people of Missouri even considered declaring border war against the state of Illinois! Instead of declaring civil war, the Prophet's enemies decided to be more clever. They formed a new political party, a secret combination like you read about in the *Book of Mormon*. They called themselves, the "Anti-Mormons." The Mormons had another name for them, "mobocrats."

In order to protect Nauvoo, policemen were called to patrol the streets and keep an eye out for any of these mobocrats. On Christmas Day, in the year 1843, the Prophet and Emma were having a Christmas Dance and Dinner at their home when a strange, haggard-looking man entered the party. At first some of the guests feared that he was a mobocrat who had come to kill or kidnap the Prophet. But as soon as the Prophet Joseph saw the dirty, tired man, he knew it was his old friend Porter Rockwell.

Porter had been imprisoned by the Missourians for six months. During that time he learned a terrible secret. A secret so terrible that the moment he was released, he rushed to tell the Prophet Joseph all about it. Simply stated it was this: one of the members of the secret combination was one of the Prophet's closest friends! This friend was part of the murder plan.

When Joseph heard the news he was devastated. He said, "I am exposed to far greater dangers from traitors among ourselves than from enemies without... All the enemies upon the face of the earth may roar and exert all their power to bring about my death, but they can accomplish nothing, unless some who are among us... join with our enemies.... We have a Judas in our midst."

It was not long before the whole town of Nauvoo and the new policemen were all watching closely to see if they could figure out which of them was the traitor. Most of the Saints were grateful for the extra police protection on the streets, but a couple of men in particular were not. The first man was named William Law and he was a member of the First Presidency, the second was William Marks, the president of the Nauvoo Stake. Another was a colonel in the Nauvoo Legion, Francis Higbee. They complained so much about the policemen watching the streets at night that the Prophet could only conclude that these men "want to prowl in the streets at pleasure without interruption." The Prophet couldn't understand their constant complaining about it. He wrote in this journal: "What can be the matter with these men? Is it that... Presidents Law and Marks are absolutely traitors to the Church... Can it be possible that the traitor whom Porter Rockwell reports to me... is a member of [the First Presidency?]"

Many secret meetings were held in and around Nauvoo by the traitors on how they might kill or capture the Prophet. At first they tried to capture him by treacherous means. William Law offered a man named Joe Jackson $500 to kill Joseph Smith.

The Saints knew Jackson as one who had wormed himself into the company and good graces of the Prophet. Jackson had worked long at this with a wicked design. He hoped to get Joseph into his power and then destroy him. Jackson had done many friendly and serviceable deeds for Joseph, and when he thought the Prophet was off his guard, he asked him out for a stroll one evening after dark.

They walked leisurely along towards the Mississippi River, talking in a friendly manner. Suddenly, Joseph stopped and turned to Jackson, saying, "I know what your design and object is tonight. Now don't take your hands out of your pockets nor make a motion like it or I will show you the power of God."

Terrible fear overcame Jackson as Joseph unveiled his sinister plan, "You have got a boat and men in readiness to kidnap me, but you will not make out to do it. You have laid your plans very cunningly, but I have known you."

Jackson left Nauvoo and never returned. With all these attempts on Joseph's life, it was decided that the Prophet needed some bodyguards. One day as the sheriff was walking down the street in Nauvoo, a window opened and one of Joseph's enemies, Francis Higbee, took aim and shot. The bullet raced through the air, striking the sheriff in the left breast. But, instead of entering his body, it fell to the ground with a thud, leaving the sheriff unharmed. The sheriff reached down, picked up the bullet and held it high towards heaven, saying, "I thank thee, O God the Eternal Father, in the name of Jesus Christ, that thou didst destroy the power of this bullet." His little son was nearby and saw it happen. Ever after he would tell his own children, "I knew then that Joseph Smith was a prophet and that my dad was right to try and protect him."

Before long it became impossible for William Law and William Marks and those other church traitors to keep their plans secret. The prophet tried to reach out in kindness to these men but as William Law would later say, "I put pistols in my pockets one night, and went to Joseph Smith's house, determined to blow his infernal brains out, but I could not get the opportunity to shoot him then, but I am determined I will shoot him the first opportunity, and you will see blood and thunder and devastation in [Nauvoo.]"

Unable to kill the Prophet, William Law decided to start a newspaper. The plan was simple. Each week they would print as many lies about the Mormons as they could, hoping to get the people of Illinois angry enough to form a mob and come down and slaughter the Saints. William Law gave the Higbees $2,000 to start the newspaper.

Soon a new press arrived from St. Louis. An advertisement was sent about the city of Nauvoo saying that a new newspaper was going to be available. This paper claimed it would expose the terrible secrets of the Mormons and would call for the State of Illinois to declare the City of Nauvoo illegal. It was called the Expositor because it was going to expose the Mormons.

The first issue of the paper was released and sent about the town. When the Saints read the terrible lies in the Expositor they were angry. Some wanted to destroy the printing press and give William Law and his associates a good beating. This was, in affect, what the Anti-Mormons wanted.

The Prophet Joseph did not fall into this trap unknowingly. After fourteen hours of discussion, the city council of Nauvoo chose to take action and declare the newspaper a public nuisance and destroy it. Joseph said that in the end he would rather die and have the lies stopped, than live and have false rumors spread about himself and the good people of the city. It was decided by legal means to stop the next printing of the Expositor. An official order was issued and the sheriff broke into the printing office and destroyed the printing press.

The Anti-Mormons wasted no time in gathering a mob at the town of Carthage. The situation became so ugly that the Governor himself came and insisted that Joseph stand trial for what he had done. The Prophet knew that if the mobs were allowed to take him again, they would kill him.

When it seemed that the mobs were going to destroy the city of Nauvoo and kill the Mormons, the Prophet Joseph decided that it was better to let them kill him and spare the Saints. So he and his brother Hyrum, along with John Taylor and Willard Richards, went to Carthage to stand trail.

On June 27th of 1844, the mob who had waited so long to kill the Prophet, rushed into the jail where he was being held and killed him and his brother Hyrum. It is said that even before news of the murders reached Nauvoo, all the animals in the city acted very strangely. Dogs howled, horses and cows bellowed in sadness and a feeling of darkness came over the people. Even though some of the mob wanted to hurry on to Nauvoo and slaughter the Saints, most of the mobocrats were satisfied--at least for a little while--by the death of Joseph and Hyrum Smith.

We could spend a lot of time talking about all the sad things that happened around this time and how the Saints were finally forced to leave in the dead of winter, only at last to come to the Valley of the Great Salt Lake. Instead, it is important for you to remember that God knew all along that this was going to happen. Some things are so important a person would rather die than see them destroyed. Is there anything in your life that is so important that you would die in order to save it? Joseph Smith felt that the Saints and the Church were that important.

Chapter Twenty Three
None Greater But the Lord Himself
(December 23rd)

Today is the Prophet Joseph Smith's birthday. Tonight makes a full circle. Over the past month we have studied the stories of our people and of our Prophet. Do you know how lucky you are to have a Prophet like Joseph Smith? Do you know how lucky you are to have modern Prophets today? Do you know who is the prophet of the church right now? Who? Say his name out loud.

We have only one more story to tell, but you don't have to stop here. If you want to learn more about Church History, there are many books available. Ask your parents to teach you more or go and get a non-fiction account and learn for yourself. Just remember this, you are very lucky to be a member of the *Church of Jesus Christ of Latter-day Saints.* Many good people have given everything they had, even their lives, so that you could be a member of this Church. Tonight in your prayers, thank your Father in Heaven for sending you living prophets today who can teach you the gospel and help you return to live in Heaven again forever with your family, your Heavenly parents and with Jesus Christ. You are very blessed and so it's good to thank God for your blessings.

There are many wonderful tributes to the Prophet Joseph Smith but none more powerful than the one written by John Taylor in the 135th Section of the *Doctrine and Covenants.* Do you have your own copy of the *Doctrine and Covenants?* If you do, turn to Section 135 and let's read it together:

Doctrine & Covenants 135:1-7 To seal the testimony of this book and the Book of Mormon, we announce the martyrdom of Joseph Smith the Prophet, and Hyrum Smith the Patriarch. They were shot in Carthage jail, on the 27th of June, 1844, about five o'clock p.m., by an armed mob — painted black — of from 150 to 200 persons. Hyrum was shot first and fell calmly, exclaiming: "I am a dead man!" Joseph leaped from the window, and was shot dead in the attempt, exclaiming: "O Lord my God!" They were both shot after they were dead, in a brutal manner, and both received four balls [meaning, bullets].

John Taylor and Willard Richards, two of the Twelve, were the only persons in the room at the time; the former was wounded in a savage manner with four balls, but has since recovered; the latter, through the providence of God, escaped, without even a hole in his robe.

Joseph Smith, the Prophet and Seer of the Lord, has done more, save Jesus only, for the salvation of men in this world, than any other man that ever lived in it. In the short space of twenty years, he has brought forth the Book of Mormon, which he translated by the gift and power of God, and has been the means of publishing it on two continents; has sent the fulness of the everlasting gospel, which it contained, to the four quarters of the earth; has brought forth the revelations and commandments which compose this book of Doctrine and Covenants, and many other wise documents and instructions for the benefit of the children of men; gathered many thousands of the Latter-day Saints, founded a great city, and left a fame and name that cannot be slain. He lived great, and he died great in the eyes of God and his people; and like most of the Lord's anointed in ancient times, has sealed his mission and his works with his own blood; and so has his brother Hyrum. In life they were not divided, and in death they were not separated!

When Joseph went to Carthage to deliver himself up to the pretended requirements of the law, two or three days previous to his assassination, he said: "I am going like a lamb to the slaughter; but I am calm as a summer's morning; I have a conscience void of offense towards God, and towards all men. I shall die innocent, and it shall yet be said of me — he was murdered in cold blood." — The same morning, after Hyrum had made ready to go — shall it be said to the slaughter? Yes, for so it was — he read the following paragraph, near the close of the twelfth chapter of *Ether*, in the *Book of Mormon*, and turned down the leaf upon it:

Ether 12:36-38 And it came to pass that I prayed unto the Lord that he would give unto the Gentiles grace, that they might have charity. And it came to pass that the Lord said unto me: If they have not charity it mattereth not unto thee, thou hast been faithful; wherefore thy garments shall be made

120

clean. *And because thou hast seen thy weakness, thou shalt be made strong, even unto the sitting down in the place which I have prepared in the mansions of my Father. And now I ... bid farewell unto the Gentiles; yea, and also unto my brethren whom I love, until we shall meet before the judgment-seat of Christ, where all men shall know that my garments are not spotted with your blood."* The testators are now dead, and their testament is in force.

Hyrum Smith was forty-four years old in February, 1844, and Joseph Smith was thirty-eight in December, 1843; and henceforward their names will be classed among the martyrs of religion; and the reader in every nation will be reminded that the *Book of Mormon*, and this book of *Doctrine and Covenants* of the church, cost the best blood of the nineteenth century to bring them forth for the salvation of a ruined world; and that if the fire can scathe a green tree for the glory of God, how easy it will burn up the dry trees to purify the vineyard of corruption. They lived for glory; they died for glory; and glory is their eternal reward. From age to age shall their names go down to posterity as gems for the sanctified.

They were innocent of any crime, as they had often been proved before, and were only confined in jail by the conspiracy of traitors and wicked men; and their innocent blood on the floor of Carthage jail is a broad seal affixed to "Mormonism" that cannot be rejected by any court on earth, and their innocent blood on the escutcheon of the State of Illinois, with the broken faith of the State as pledged by the governor, is a witness to the truth of the everlasting gospel that all the world cannot impeach; and their innocent blood on the banner of liberty, and on the magna charta of the United States, is an ambassador for the religion of Jesus Christ, that will touch the hearts of honest men among all nations; and their innocent blood, with the innocent blood of all the martyrs under the altar that John saw, will cry unto the Lord of Hosts till he avenges that blood on the earth. Amen.

I can only add my testimony that Joseph Smith Jr., was a prophet of the Lord Jesus Christ. That because of his faithful stewardship in restoring the church, you and I can once again enjoy all of the blessings possible for God's children on earth. Do you have a testimony of Joseph Smith? What do you think? Take a moment and share your thoughts and feelings with your family. Testimonies grow when shared and it's always wonderful to know that you have friends and family who also know that the *Church of Jesus Christ of Latter-day Saints* is true. *The End*

Joseph Smith, Jr. the Prophet of the Lord

This is the only photograph of the Prophet Joseph Smith, Jr., verified by his immediate family as being actually him. His eldest son Joseph Smith III registered this image as a photograph of his father in order to safeguard the copyright.

BONUS CHAPTER

The Joseph Smith Daguerrotype
Was the Prophet Photographed?

The photograph on the left is a copy of an original daguerreotype taken of Joseph Smith Jr. in Nauvoo just before his death in 1844. It has caused a lot of excitement among researchers who study the image of the Prophet Joseph Smith.

The Prophet's son, Joseph Smith III, submitted this photographic copy of his father's daguerreotype to the Library of Congress in 1879.[2] A daguerreotype is a small unique photographic image that can only be duplicated by being re-photographed.[3] Clear reproduction presented a challenge because the majority of daguerreotypes in 1844 were only the size of a large postage stamp.[4] The Library of Congress copy on the cover is an 8x10 inch print, which would be an obvious enlargement of a small original daguerreotype.[5]

This 1879 duplication was done with film and equipment that by today's standards would seem quite primitive. It has been retouched around the hair, coat, on the cravat-or necktie-and the vest. Joseph's pompadour hairstyle, considered fashionable at the time[6], has been poorly frisked or masked along the outline.[7] This retouching has caused the loss of softer, finer, transitional hair between the parted sections.[8] Joseph's face seems free of any artistic retouching, but there is an overall "grainy" quality that causes the image to be less than one might expect from a photograph.[9] This "graininess" is probably due to the gross enlargement from the original daguerreotype, however there is a startling photographic quality to the eyes.[10]

This photo may be all that is left of the original image, as the daguerreotype has not been found. It was good that Joseph's son saw the need to safeguard his father's photograph with this copy so that over 150 years later we can now see what Joseph Smith really looked like.

It is believed by a few that this photograph is merely a painting. Careful study of the data compiled by experts shows this belief to be incorrect. Much excitement has come from the comparative studies of this image and a death mask made of the Prophet just after his death. Experts in Facial Surgery, Forensic Pathology, Plastic and Facial Reconstruction, Art, Art History, Archival and Photographic History have put together information that not only substantiates the photographic nature of this image, but sheds new light on the history of Joseph Smith in a unique and extraordinary way [11]

DETAILS IN THE PHOTOGRAPH REVEAL CLUES TO JOSEPH'S EXPERIENCES

Photography was first introduced in 1839 by a man named Louis-Jacques-Mandé Daguerre. Therefore, examples of this new technology were called daguerreotypes.[12] History shows us that a photographer trained in this art named Lucien R. Foster, moved to Nauvoo in 1844 and lived with the Prophet Joseph at the Nauvoo Mansion.[13] Brother Foster was a branch president in New York City and after moving to Nauvoo, was given responsibilities by the Prophet.[14]

Joseph was murdered on the 27th day of June, 1844. The following August, L.R. Foster moved out of the Mansion to a daguerreotype studio on Main Street. During the time all

Fig. 1: The RLDS painting. This is the painting that Joseph III stated looked the most like his father. It is important to note that Joseph III stated this painting was created the same year that his father had his picture taken. This portrait was painted from the daguerreotype. He further said that this painting most closely resembled his father and his father's photograph. This has lead many to believe that this portrait was painted from the photograph.

Nauvoo was mourning the loss of their dear "departed friend" the Prophet Joseph, Foster began advertising an exhibition of his daguerreotypes. Curiously, part of his exhibit was at the late Prophet's home. It is logical that the daguerreotype of Joseph was displayed there since records state it belonged to the Smith Family.[15] Mr. Foster states in his advertisement:

How valuable or rather invaluable, would be such a likeness of an absent or departed friend. Specimens may be seen ...at the Nauvoo Mansion.[16]

Joseph Smith III remembered Lucien Foster taking a picture of his father. Later in his life, Joseph III would state that he owned the most accurate oil portrait of Joseph Smith in existence. (see Fig. 1) He based this assertion on the fact that the painting was "sustained" in its likeness by the daguerreotype.[17] Since Joseph Smith III copyrighted the daguerreotype, we will refer to the photograph as the "JS Photograph" and to the oil portrait which resembles it as the "RLDS painting" to lessen confusion when discussing them.

Over the years, scholars have thought that several photographs of Joseph were taken from the RLDS painting. This painting offers striking resemblance to the JS Photograph. In fact experts believe the painting must have been drawn from the JS Photograph. Consider Joseph III's statement, "It fortunately happens to us that this portrait [RLDS painting]...is sustained...by the daguerreotype in our possession."[18]

The resemblance between these two images is not coincidental. Art authorities say, of all the depictions of the Prophet, this is the only painting that reflects unusual talent, showing an uncommon frontal view that would be very difficult for any artist associated with the Prophet to accomplish in such a well proportioned way.[19] However, through the assistance of a photograph, even an average artist might paint an image of this quality.

The use of the photography as an aid to art was, and still is, a common practice. In the mid 1800s, portraits painted from photographic images were considered more valuable than the photographs themselves and understandably so, because the photograph revealed the true nature of the subject's face with all his flaws, scars, asymmetry, etcetera. On the other hand, paintings make a person look better and more dignified. They are also more costly to produce. They were also in color. Photography was sort of a "poor man's" art, since it was affordable to the common people. Consequently we have numerous 19th century photographs of people from all walks of life, exposing them as they really looked and lived.[20]

It is the perfect reflection of nature found in photographs that intrigued the experts examining the JS Photograph. It exhibits many natural details that artists avoid when painting. Listed below are some of the more interesting findings, not only from the Art and Photographic experts, but from Medical experts as well.[21] Notice:

1. There is an asymmetrical quality to the face caused in part by the depressed maxillary area of the left cheek. (see Fig. 6)

Fig. 2: On the left side of the cupid's bow, just above the lip, there is evidence of a scar in the JS Photograph.

2. There is an apparent scar with swelling on the Prophet's upper left eyelid and a hint of a scar on the upper lip. (see Figs.2 & 6)

3. Certain areas of the photograph, especially the eyes, have a very photographic, optically correct appearance. Enlargements of the eyes reveal eyelashes and hints of blood vessels as well as other small anatomical details. (see Fig.3)

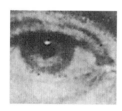

Fig. 3: The right eye of the Prophet. Note the blood vessels in the whites of his eyes.

4. The iris of the eyes reveal detail so minute that even an accurate pupillary reflex to light is evident and measurable. Joseph's left pupil is exposed to more light than his right and has reacted by constricting to become 25% smaller.

5. Maxillo-Facial Surgeons indicate that Joseph's scar and swelling of his upper left eyelid are evidence of a striking blow to that side of his face resulting in the trauma evident in the JS Photograph. The scar on his upper lip may have come from the beating he took at the Johnson home when he was dragged out of bed in the middle of the night by a mob. They flogged, tarred

and feathered him. Then a bottle of nitric acid was forced into his closed mouth. The bottle cut his lip and chipped a tooth, but they failed to accomplish their evil designs.[22]

6. The button visible at the bottom right of the JS Photograph has an out of focus, three dimensional, and extremely realistic, photographic quality. (see Fig 4.)

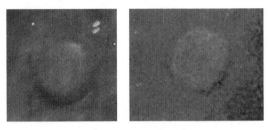

Fig. 4: <u>Left</u>: A button taken from the JS Photograph. This button is out of focus due to the principle of depth of field. Such a phenomenon occurs naturally when three-dimensional objects are photographed. This was very common with daguerreotypes due to the single aperture setting. <u>Right</u>: The corresponding button on the RLDS painting. Notice that this is obviously a painted button.

7. An expert in clothing styles and textiles found the weave of the fabric in an enlargement of the area around the left collar and lapel. This weave was found to be in the directions appropriate to the different cuts of this style of clothing. The clothing detail and weave of the fabric would be too tedious for an artist to paint. This expert also noted what appears to be repair stitching next to the button. She stated that this stitch occurs in just the right place to repair damage caused if someone were to grab Joseph forcefully by the buttoned collar and lapel.

8. On the Prophet's coat there are many tiny details not readily perceived by the naked eye. One can see the two button holes on his left lapel, but what is not so obvious is a small button hole found when the upper lapel area is magnified. A clothing expert said there should be a small button hole there, and indeed,

when the area was enlarged, there was. It is hard to imagine a painter of Joseph's day caring about a tiny and nearly invisible button hole.

9. Photographs reveal the true nature of a person's face. They show every face is composed of two different sides. This difference can be illustrated when you view a mirror or reversed image of a familiar face. The reversed image, because you are not used to it, will look strange and possibly out of balance. To demonstrate this, look at the photograph in a mirror. This shocking effect is less noticeable when viewing reversed images of Joseph's painted portraits because painters tend to clean up asymmetry and remove facial flaws, giving people more symmetrical appearances.

10. Unquestionably there is a great deal of hand painting, retouching, or other rendering involved in this photo. The odd outline of Joseph's hair looks as if a stencil, frisket, mask or blocking device was used. It is very clumsy and unconvincing, and it is the type of masking which would more logically be done in painting a photographic print than in creating a wholly non-photographic painting: it definitely produces an effect which one finds in painted nineteenth-century photographic prints.

11. The JS Photograph exhibits the photographic principle of depth of field. Note the image is in focus at the center and becomes progressively out of focus the farther one looks from the focal plane. The eyes and face are in focus but the shoulders are out of the focal length of the lens and are therefore out of focus. This illustrates the three dimensional aspect of the subject. In other words, the source of this image was not a two dimensional flat object-like a painting-but a real physical object (i.e. a man). The button on Joseph's left demonstrates this three dimensional,

out of focus quality as well. It looks like a real button, not a painted one.

12. The white shirt and tie (cravat) are overexposed, as is common in photographs of the period. This happened because early photographers could only approximate the exposure time, therefore light areas of a photograph were commonly overexposed and had to be retouched in order to bring out the shadows and form. This cravat has been retouched and is the only area where brush strokes can be found.

A COMPARISON WITH THE DEATH MASK

Shortly after the death of the Prophet Joseph Smith Jr., a mold of plaster was made of his face.[23] This death mask has been studied and considered by some to be the most accurate image of him, setting it up as a "litmus test" for checking the accuracy of any image of the Prophet.[24] The mask has been compared to the many images of Joseph Smith, as well as the JS Photograph on the cover. The photo does not match the death mask in some very interesting areas. A comparison of the two images shows that the death mask has a more elongated area from the tip of the nose to the end of the chin. Specifically, the "cupids bow" or the portion of the upper lip just under the nose, is wider and fuller in the death mask. (see Fig. 5)

Despite this elongated area, there are more similarities than differences. Plastic and Facial Surgeons, a Forensic Pathologist and a Mortician examined a plaster copy of the death mask. One of the experts stated that if the death mask were a fraud, its copy source must have been the JS Photograph, since the two images are so similar.[25] Some of the features common to both images, as stated by these experts, are listed below: (see Fig. 6)

Fig. 5: The area of greatest difference between the JS Photograph and the Death mask is the lower third of the face. Joseph III felt that he death mask was too prominent, or elongated, in this area. This is the area that does not pass the "litmus" test by those who insist that all images must line up perfectly with the mask in order to be called authentic. New research explains that, in fact, this particular area should be longer than any photographic image.

1. The depressed maxillary area of the left cheek.

2. The apparent scar on the upper lip (left side of the "cupids bow").

3. A horizontally straight scar on the upper left eye-lid.

4. A swelling of the upper left eye-lid in the photo, with the accompanying death dehydration of that area on the death mask.

5. The shape of the chin and jaw are nearly identical (except for the more elongated position on the mask).

6. Overall facial dimensions such as the distance from the brow to hairline, the curve and lengths of the eyebrows, the shape of the nose, the distance between the eyes and the shape of the lips, etc.

As mentioned previously, it may be interesting for the reader to note that Joseph Smith's history of repeated beatings coupled with his reputation as an expert wrestler may account for items 1-4. The scar on the upper lip (more apparent in the photograph), may be evidence of the night a bottle of poison was forced into his mouth by a mob, cutting the upper lip and breaking a tooth.[26]

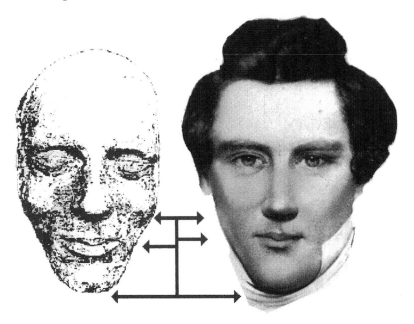

Fig. 6A: <u>Left</u>: The death mask of Joseph Smith. <u>Right</u>: The JS Photograph. Note the important similarities and differences. All of these are consistent with historic and biographic data. Each supports the veracity of the other.

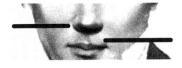

Fig. 6B: <u>Left</u>: In the photograph, Joseph's left cheek is lower than his right one. Probably from an injury. The artistic images of the Prophet correct this human flaw. Such subtleties do not escape the camera's eye.

Fig. 6C: <u>Right</u>: The left eye shows evidence of chronic swelling and a horizontal scar just below the eye-brow.

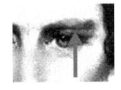

As stated the similarities greatly out weight the differences, however the question must be asked, "Why is there a difference between these two images?" First of all it has been established historically and by various experts that the JS Photograph is authentic[27], and we accepted that the death mask was probably legitimate.[28] Experts state that any differences between the two are minor and could be explained by the angle of the photograph or by some death changes in the mask.[29] However, we felt that the difference of elongation in the lower part of the face, in the mask, was significant.

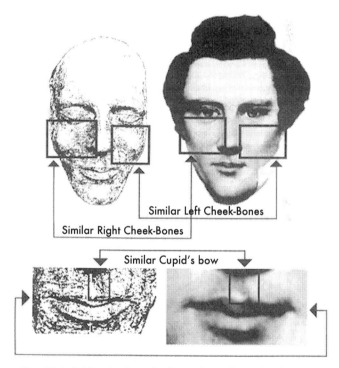

Fig. 6D: <u>Left</u>: The death mask of Joseph Smith. <u>Right</u>: The JS Photograph. <u>Note</u>: Top: Identical similarity in cheek structure between the Death Mask and the JS Photograph. Bottom: Identical similarity between lip-scar and lip-line of the two images.

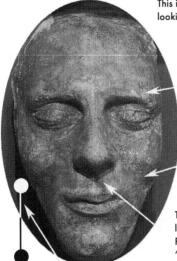

Fig. 6E: The Death Mask of Joseph Smith Jr. This illustration is best used as a guide when looking at the three dimensional mask.

Notice the scar and dehydrated area of the left eye lid. Compare this same area in the JS Photograph. This is more obvious when viewed on the three dimensional mask.

Possible depressed fractured cheek. This can also be seen in the JS Photograph.

This the area under the nose – the upper lip – is wider, or thicker, than in the JS Photograph. The apparent scar in the "cupid's bow" region of the upper lip matches the photograph well. Again, this scar is easier to see when viewed in three dimension on the actual mask at the LDS Church History Museum.

This is the area of elongation or "prominence" that represents the greatest difference between the JS Photograph and the Mask. It is the area that Joseph III said was "too prominent" and therefore the most unlike his father's natural appearance. Additional information dealing with this difference follow.

To explain this difference, it was necessary to get all the information related to the mask, the death of the Prophet and any facial changes that could have occurred after death. We found a whole new area of study that answers many questions and helps substantiate not only the photograph, but the death mask as well. The following is a brief explanation of this new area of study and its findings.

The Skull — the Missing Link

While researching the death of Joseph Smith Jr., we came across information that he, and his brother Hyrum, were exhumed, examined and photographed in 1928 by the RLDS church.[30] Out of respect for the Prophet, the RLDS Church has refused to allow these pictures to be published.[31] However, the authors received permission from the RLDS Church to have these exhumation photographs studied by a team of experts in Forensic Pathology, Anthropology and Facial Trauma.[32] Years ago, detailed tracings from the skull photos were made by Utah artist William Whitaker. These will be used here to illustrate the findings of the experts.

A study of the RLDS exhumation photographs show that Joseph's skull is missing the facial area. (see Fig. 7) That his bones were missing was made even more puzzling when we found that

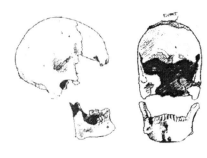

Fig. 7A: Left: The remains of the skull of Joseph Smith Jr., traced by William Whitaker from the photographs taken by the RLDS during the Prophet's exhumation in 1928. Notice that the Prophet is missing his facial bones. Previously it has been assumed that this void resulted from decomposition in the grave. Our evidence reveals a different conclusion.

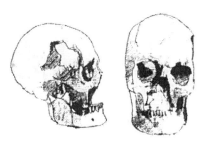

Fig. 7B: Left: The remains of the skull of Hyrum Smith. If one assumes that the only explanation for the void in Joseph's skull (see Fig. 7A) is decomposition, then the fact that his bones are missing is made even more puzzling when we consider two things. First, that Hyrum's facial bones are intact even through he was shot through the face at the time of his death, and second, Hyrum was buried right next to Joseph, therefore decomposition alone cannot account for Joseph's missing bone structure.

his brother Hyrum's facial bones were intact, even though he was shot in the face at the time of his death.[33] We therefore considered that when Joseph the Prophet fell from the second story window at Carthage Jail in June of 1844, he suffered facial fractures. Because death occurred only minutes after this event, the bones never healed together, and as decomposition of the soft tissues progressed in the grave, the fragments fell from the face, leaving a void in the skull.

DID JOSEPH RECEIVE FACIAL FRACTURES?

We will need to return to history for a moment to answer this question. There are several eyewitness accounts recording that Joseph fell on his head/face from the second story of the Carthage Jail. (see Fig. 8)

Fig. 8: An artistic rendering of the martyrdom of Joseph Smith at Carthage Jail. Note that the Prophet is falling out head (or face) first.

These eyewitness stories are told from different perspectives that sometimes contradict each other, but always there are common elements.

One of the most consistent aspects of these stories is that Joseph fell or jumped out of the Carthage jail window head first, landing on his head/face and then, as if that weren't enough, he was hit in the face. The first account is from Willard

Richards who was in the room with Joseph when he went out of the window.:

Joseph attempted, as the last resort, to leap [out] the same window from whence Mr. Taylor fell, when two balls pierced him from the door, and one entered his right breast from without, and he fell outward, exclaiming,-"Oh Lord, my God!" As [Joseph's] feet went out of the window my head went in, the balls whistling all around. He fell on his left side a dead man.[34]

When we compare the Richards's accounts to the next few, it will become obvious that his feet went out last or in other words he went out head first, falling on the ground below.

The second account is from Wm. M. Daniels, an eyewitness. It was published by John Taylor for the Proprietor in Nauvoo, in 1845:

He seemed to fall easy and struck partly on his right shoulder and back, his neck and head reaching the ground a little before his feet. He rolled instantly on his face. From this position he was taken by a young man, who sprang to him from the other side of the fence, who held a pewter knife in his hand ...[35]

The young man with "a pewter knife in his hand" was William Webb. Mr. Webb gives a testimony of his version of the death that may give another reason for the fractured condition of the Prophet's skull:

The door flew open; I saw two men in the room. We shot at them several times; at length one of them fell on the floor; the other [Joseph Smith] jumped out of the window. I ran down the stairs to see where he was. When I got to him he was trying to get up. He appeared stunned by the fall. I struck him in the face and said: "Old Jo, damn you, where are you now!" I then set him up against the well-curb and went away from him. Signed, Wm. Webb[36]

Another eyewitness mentions how he saw Webb strike Joseph in the face:

It seems to me [Joseph] came out head first, and he was shot while passing through the window... [On the ground] I think he raised himself to a sitting position. A young man went up and struck him either with the end of his gun or a bayonet.[37]

Several of these accounts also state that after he was hit in the face by Webb, the mob shot him and he fell over on his face again, "a dead man."

Did the Prophet Joseph receive facial fractures at the time of his death? The historical record shows that he received more than enough trauma to cause facial fractures. When you combine the historical probability of trauma, with the fractured condition of the skull as it was found in 1928, one must concluded, as the Pathologist concluded, "You can come to no other conclusion than he must have fractured his face at the time of his death."[38]

FACIAL FRACTURES EXPLAIN THE DIFFERENCES BETWEEN THE DEATH MASK AND THE JS PHOTOGRAPH

The experts in facial fractures and trauma point out that it is no coincidence that the death mask is different from the JS Photograph. The aforementioned areas on the mask are just those areas that change the appearance of a person when they receive the kind of facial fractures that are present in the skull of Joseph Smith. This explains why the mask is dimensionally different from the photograph in those areas.

For many people it also explains why the drawings and paintings of the Prophet, done from the death mask, are incompatible with the countless handsome personal descriptions given of the Prophet. Some of the side profiles done by these artists may reflect the fractured distorted face from the death mask. When the chin is brought foreword by some artists in their sculptures and drawings, it is probably done to make him look more handsome. In deviating from the death mask template, artists are inadvertently correcting the image, making him look more like we now think he did.

As one refers to medical textbooks on facial fractures and consults with Facial Trauma Surgeons, the descriptions fit, "to a tee," the area in question on both the mask and the skull. To facial trauma experts, there are well known areas of the face that fracture when a person receives a blow to the face. These areas of "breakage" occur along natural fault lines called "suture" lines in the bones of the skull. The lines specific to Joseph Smith's trauma are called the Le Forte I, II, and III fracture lines. (see Fig. 9)

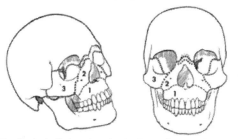

Fig. 9: A skull showing the Le Forte fracture lines.

When the bones associated with the Le Forte lines break they can sometimes become displaced, moving in the soft tissues of the face. This bone displacement causes a person's face to look different. In fact, Le Forte fractures are characterized by the person's face becoming elongated. Joseph Smith's skull and death mask present the classic signs of the Le Forte fractures. The elongated face of the mask is evident, as we have stated, when compared to the JS Photograph. Even the widened area of the upper lip on the mask, as compared to the photo, can be explained by displacement of the Le Forte I fracture line. (see Fig. 10 on following page)

There is also physical evidence in the death mask, and a mention in the historical record, that the Prophet's nose was stuffed with cotton. This was probably done for several reasons:

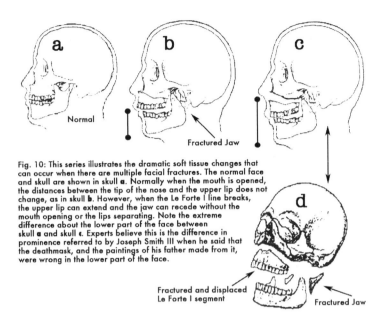

Fig. 10: This series illustrates the dramatic soft tissue changes that can occur when there are multiple facial fractures. The normal face and skull are shown in skull **a**. Normally when the mouth is opened, the distances between the tip of the nose and the upper lip does not change, as in skull **b**. However, when the Le Forte I line breaks, the upper lip can extend and the jaw can recede without the mouth opening or the lips separating. Note the extreme difference about the lower part of the face between skull **a** and skull **c**. Experts believe this is the difference in prominence referred to by Joseph Smith III when he said that the deathmask, and the paintings of his father made from it, were wrong in the lower part of the face.

Skulls **c** and **d** show the fractured and displaced Le Forte I segment from different angles. Skull **d** shows the skull removed from the face with the fracture labeled for clarity.

Fig. 10B: <u>Right</u>: Joseph Smith's death mask in profile with a representational fractured skull. This illustration shows the displaced bone fractures that created the image preserved in the dead mask. Difference seen between the JS photo and the mask, combined with the evidence found in 1928 skull, demonstrates he must have broken and displaced the Le Forte I and jaw. The skull evidence also shows the possibility of fractured Le Forte II and III segments. When this evidence is applied to a generic skull and then placed in the death mask, as we see here, a picture emerges that explains why the mask image is distorted when compared to the photograph.

1. Cotton packing would keep the plaster out of the nose when making the death mask.

2. It may have been used to pack the nose and help splint the fractured distorted face into a more normal position. This kind of packing to splint and support fractures is still used today.

3. It prevented body fluids from leaking out. The historical record indicates cotton was used on both Hyrum's and Joseph's bodies for this purpose, so as to prepare them for viewing.[39]

Medical texts state that leaking cerebral-spinal fluid from the nose is a classic sign of LeForte facial trauma. The packing of the nose could have been done to stop this rather gory symptom for the body's public viewing. However, regardless of the reason, it would also push down on the Le-Forte I fracture and cause a greater displacement of the maxilla (upper teeth.) This would easily account for the elongated area of the upper lip [see Fig. 10] and therefore the retrognathic condition of the lower face (i.e. the extremely recessed lower jaw). As one can see, facial trauma gives numerous rationale for the differences between the death mask and the Prophet's living image, the JS Photograph.

JOSEPH SMITH III KNEW

Returning to history for a moment, we find an interesting description of the death mask by Joseph Smith Jr's son, Joseph Smith III. He knew his father, lived with his father, and was nearly 12 years old when his father died. Certainly he knew as well as anyone what his father looked like. Joseph III may not have known about his father's facial fractures, but he definitely had a problem with the distortions created by them when artists reproduced his father's image using the death mask. He said:

...the expression about the lower part of the face, taken from the death mask, which I saw reproduced in Ogden... several years ago, gives too full prominence to the lips and chin."39[40]

Now that new light has been shed, may we consider this photo for what Joseph Smith's son, and our experts say it is, an Actual Photograph of Joseph Smith the Prophet.

A LITTLE MORE

The former summation was prepared for a 1994 meeting in Nauvoo, Illinois commemorating the 150th anniversary of the Prophet and Patriarch's martyrdom at Carthage Jail. It was taken from the longer work: *Photograph Found: A Concise History of the Joseph Smith Daguerreotype.* Anyone wishing more details is encouraged to read that book. In the 1990s, the major controversy with the JS Photograph was that it did not <u>exactly</u> match the prophet's death mask and that many believed it was merely a photograph of the RLDS painting. Much of our research's minutiae resulted from these two arguments.

Since the release of that document, a few additional studies have been undertaken which help prove the validity of our arguments in favor of the photograph, as well as, Joseph Smith III's statement that the RLDS painting was actually painted from the photograph. Here are some of the highlights of that additional research.

PAINTINGS MADE FROM PHOTOGRAPHS IN JOSEPH'S NAUVOO

Photography had not been invented long, when painters saw its usefulness as a medium to capture subjects accurately. Prior to photography, an artist would have a sitting and sketch a model from life, or would use a life or death mask of the person in question. Early Mormon photographic expert Nelson Wadsworth long suspected that artist William Major was the one

Fig. 11 <u>Left</u>: The RLDS painting of Joseph Smith, drawn from the Foster Daguerreotype. <u>Right</u>: The photograph of the Prophet which Joseph Smith III deposited at the Library of Congress in order to secure its copyright. For clarity, this photo is herein referred to as the JS Photograph.

responsible for the famous (and much loved) painting of Joseph Smith herein referred to as the RLDS paining. (see Fig. 11)

Major was baptized into the church in London in 1842. In August of 1844, he emigrated to Nauvoo, Illinois, where he "soon became acquainted with the Authorities of the Church, and was extensively employed by them in his profession, that of an artist." It was during this same month that Lucien Foster advertised his daguerreotype rooms and mentioned that samples of his work could be seen at the Nauvoo Mansion. Major could have easily viewed the Prophet's photograph at that time. Major was interested in painting Joseph Smith. He is listed as painting *another* portrait of the Prophet in the *History of the Church*. Brigham Young recorded on April 4th, 1845: "Brother William W. Major exhibited a painting of the assassination of Joseph and Hyrum Smith by the mob at Carthage."

It is known that Major used photography to as means of creating art. Wadsworth found evidence that Major used a daguerreotype of Brigham Young to paint a portrait of him. While the original daguerreotype of Young has been lost, we have an engraving that was taken from it. (see Fig. 12) By overlaying the engraving, on top of the painting, Wadsworth showed that — while the images were not exactly the same — the major facial lines were precise. (see Fig. 13) Using the same technique, we overlaid the JS photograph and the RLDS painting. We observed the same phenomenon with the exception that the facial lines are not as precise. (see Fig. 14)

In order to paint such accurate lines, Major would have used a device like the "portable camera obscura" or the "camera lucida." Note that there are some interesting changes Major made between the Brigham Young painting and the engraving he used to produce it. These can also be seen in the Joseph Smith images. This circumstantial evidence suggests Major did paint the RLDS painting from the JS photograph. These similarities are:

1-Both original images have a blank background while the paintings have an elaborate background setting.

2-Both paintings turn the subject slightly to his right.

3-Both paintings downplay the more "casual stance" found in the originals.

4-Both paintings lengthen the collar on the subject's left side, giving the portrait a "statelier" appearance.

5-Both paintings reposition the hands. (There are no hands in the JS photo, while one is introduced in the RLDS painting.)

Fig. 12: Two images of Brigham Young. <u>Left</u>: William Major's painting of Brigham Young. <u>Right</u>: An engraving of Young made from a known but currently missing daguerreotype by Marsena Cannon.

Fig. 13: <u>Left</u>: The Wm. Major Painting overlaid with the engraving. Nelson Wadsworth found that Major used Cannon's daguerreotype to paint President Young. It was a common practice for artists to use photography to add realism to their work. We believe that the JS Photograph has been used several times to create art work of Joseph Smith. In creating his painting of Young, Major altered several aspects from the original photo.

A comparison between the RLDS painting and the JS photograph reveal the same alteration. We believe that William Major painted the RLDS painting from the JS photograph. See Fig. 14.

Fig 14: Outline of the JS Photograph (thinner line) overlaid with the outline of the RLDS painting (thicker line). While the imagines are similar they are not identical. These same changes can be observed in Major's use of Brigham Young's daguerreotype to create his painting.

6-Both paintings introduce a ring on the subject's hand where none appears in the photographs. (There is no hand in the JS photo, while a hand with a ring on it is introduced in the RLDS painting.)

Given similarities in artistic technique, the historical association of Major to the painting, and the historical evidence of a Mormon painter named William Major living in Nauvoo, we believe that William Major did paint the RLDS painting. We also believe that he used the JS Photograph as his "crutch".

Further evidence of this can be seen from a known painting by William Major in the LDS Church's collection, known as: *In Nauvoo 1843 - 1844, Joseph and Friends.* (see Fig. 15) It contains many prominent LDS figures seated while being addressed by Joseph Smith. What immediately strikes one about this painting is that

Fig. 15: In Nauvoo 1843 - 1844, Joseph and Friends, by William Major. American Art was still coming into its own in the 1800's. William Major's painting of Joseph Smith (standing) with various early church leaders of note. Notice how each is posed differently. Interestingly enough, Major used known photographs or other "crutches" to capture the various individual likenesses.

every figure included is posed as if they alone make up their own painting. None of the figures seem even interested in Joseph's speech, nor are they looking at him.

It quickly becomes apparent that each figure was painted using a separate photograph. Now you know his technique, look at William Major's painting above. The painting clearly illustrates his use of photography and other previously conceived sketches to create art. Many of the figures portrayed have known corresponding photographs.[41] Lastly, there is conclusive evidence from within the Prophet's family at Nauvoo that the practice of using photographs to paint portraits was indeed done. During the 1950's while refurbishing Joseph Smith's Mansion House in

Fig. 15: A very fragile oil painting found in the attic of Joseph Smith's Mansion House in Nauvoo during a 1950's refurbishing. The identity of the woman was unknown until Lachlan Mackay discovered her identity. He, in connection with RLDS archivist Ronald Romig authenticated it, publishing their findings publicly in 2005. This black and white copy was given to the authors by the RLDS Archive in 1993. Copyrighted by the Community of Christ church, used here under the US Copyright Fair Use Clause, please see notes for legal rationale.

Nauvoo, Sidney Moore, an antique dealer and artist discovered a deteriorating oil painting in the Prophet's attic (see Fig. 15). Little to nothing was known of the woman in the painting until 1992 when at the death of the Prophet's great-grandson, another member of the Smith family, Lachlan MacKay, was sorting through family artifacts in the attic. There he found a packet of old photographs labeled, "Mother Smith's Pictures." Lachlan was very surprised to discover that one of the photographs resembled the rotting painting to a stunning degree (see Fig. 16).

Together with **RLDS** Archivist Ronald Romig, they were successfully able to prove beyond any reasonable doubt that they had discovered the only know photograph of Joseph and Hyrum's mother, Lucy Mack Smith. The authors met with Lachlan and Ron Romig shortly after their discovery. They were very kind in showing us high quality reproductions of both the painting and the photograph. Figure 15 is the copy we were

Fig. 16: The only known photograph of Lucy Mack Smith, mother of the Prophet Joseph and Patriarch Hyrum Smith. It was discovered by Lachlan Mackay in a Smith family attic and authenticated with the aid of RLDS Archivist Ronald Romig. *This picture is copyrighted by the Community of Christ church, used here under the Fair Use Clause of US Copyright Law. Rationale for Fair Use is made in the note section.* Notice the obvious use of this photograph as the "crutch" for the corresponding painting. This discovery adds enormous weight to Joseph Smith III's contention that his father's famous painting strongly resembled his father's photograph.

given at that time. While we were extremely interested in this new find, our excitement was anchored in a different port. We believed at the time that this new discovery added significant weight to our contention that some artist, likely William Major, used Joseph Smith's photograph to paint the RDLS painting of him. The fact that a painting had been found in the attic of Joseph Smith's residence which was clearly done from a photograph seemed to us to be the final nail in a perfect coffin!

We asked the RLDS for permission to include this data in our forth-coming document. Ronald asked us not to, and so out of respect to him, Lachlan and the christian kindness with which we were treated by the RLDS, we left all mention of this out of our documents at the time. In the Fall of 2005, Romig and Lachlan released these images and their findings publicly.[42] Normally newly discovered images such as these can be protected by copyright, however, because their findings dovetail with our research, we have the right to reproduce them under the *Fair Use Clause* of United States Copyright Law. Our legal reasonings can be found in the note section.

Using the same technique as Wadsworth's Brigham Young imagery comparison (see Figs. 12 & 13, previous) and our similar study of the JS Photograph to the RLDS Painting (see Fig. 14, previous) we made a similar comparison of these new images. Once again the findings strongly suggest that an artist used photography to portray prominent Nauvoo Smiths. This was not only an advantage to the artist, who had a consistently precise model, it was also nice for the model who could hand a photograph to the painter and then walk away.[43] Our comparison illustrates the likelihood that the artist set his focal plane on Lucy's nose and radiated outward (see Fig. 17). The painting appears to differ more and more in concentric circles away from the center of her face. We also believe, based on the comparison, that the painting was not finished although as to the reason we can only speculate.

The fact the Lucy spent her final years living at the Mansion House with her daughter-in-law Emma, combined with the discovery of the painting in the attic, further makes our case for the RLDS painting being exactly what Joseph Smith III said it was: the most accurate painting of his father and based on a photograph. We consider Lucy's photograph and subsequent painting to be vindication of his statement.

Fig. 17: An overlay comparison of Lucy Mack Smith's photograph and painting. Note the near perfect alignment of the nose and mouth crease with slight but increasing variations radiating outward. Further, the photograph had to be slightly elongated as well. Such a pattern is consistent with lens type re-projections suggesting the use of a *camera lucida* or *camera obscura*. Both techniques were possible and consistent with practices at the time. This discovery validates Joseph III's claim about his father's painting being made from a photograph in the family's possession.

Lastly, there had been some debate near the turn of the millenium that perhaps the exhumed skulls of Joseph and Hyrum were accidentally mislabeled when they were exhumed from the grave. We brought this question to various experts in forensic medicine who gave their opinion that the skulls had not been mislabeled. Joseph's skull shows all the signs of blunt force trauma consistent with a fall from a second story window while Hyrum's skull shows all of the signs of a bullet entrance and exit wound on the right side of his nose. (see Fig 18) Anyone suggesting that the skulls should be switched need to show when Hyrum fell from a second story window and when Joseph was shot in the face. In short, the skulls have not been mislabeled.

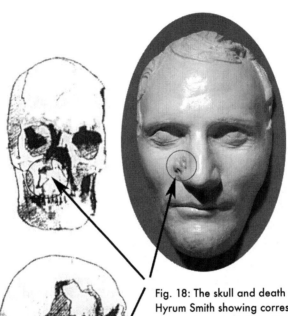

Fig. 18: The skull and death mask of Hyrum Smith showing corresponding bullet entry points on all three. These match perfectly with forensics, history and eye-witness accounts. Anyone suggesting that this skull is Joseph's instead of Hyrum's must also consider that Hyrum's mask above, is really Joseph. The problem is that this is not Joseph's death mask, it's Hyrum's.

Rationale for Fair Use of Copyrighted Items Herein

We acknowledge that some of the images included in this document are owned and still under copyright protection by others, namely, the Community of Christ Church which is also still legally known as the Reorganized Church of Jesus Christ of Latter-day Saints (which has no official affiliation with the Utah headquartered Church of Jesus Christ of Latter-day Saints, other than friendship.) United States Copyright Law allows authors, scholars, educators, newsmen and others to use, publish and reproduce another's copyrighted works without permission under certain guidelines. Since courts have judged each use on their own merits, it has become a common practice to show an intended Fair Use Claim to a 3rd-party (usually an attorney) for an opinion. While not required to do so, we have followed this practice and included the findings here.

Again, while NOT required to do so, we have listed our reasons for fair using these images under the claim of Fair Use solely to show that our intentions are not to offend but merely to educate. We have nothing but respect for our historical colleagues and hope the following rationales will demonstrate that (as well as soften feelings, if possible.)

The law allows Fair Use when copyrighted material is being used to make a specific educational, research-based, scholarly, and/or critical comment on the work used. This is needed in free society since knowledge and history could not advance if copyright holders had the right to refuse use for any reason. They would therefore be able to control knowledge which is counter-productive to truth. In careful consultation with our attorney, we were informed that we met ALL of the above uses in each of the items used. Any ONE alone is sufficient for use.

Fair Use is also legal when it causes a "transformative" effect on the work, meaning that it changes the work to serve a new purpose. Visually our use here does this, particularly figures 15 - 17. Here we have "transformed" the historical meaning of the works as important illustrations of photographic-painterly history in Nauvoo as well as gives these images the "added" meaning of being connected to Smith Family imagery in its larger context of creation, providence, and etc.

The Law further allows Fair Use when items used are "factually-based, non-fiction or news-worthy" to the public. We believe this point is obvious in our case. In connection, if the item was previously published, the claim is strengthened. As already mentioned these items were released, with proper credit given over ten years ago (as of our use in 2017.) Fair Use is also legally permissible if the use does not cause the copyright holder to lose the use-value of the work. In order to strengthen our already strong claim here, we have released these images at a lower resolution then we have access to and in "grey-scale" in order to make the originals more valuable and desirable for future release by the copyright owners, in the event they wish to do so. Lastly courts have said that it is not a limiting factor as to whether the use is included in a "for-profit venture." This is logical as all scholarly and news-worthy releases are connected to profit more or less.

Courts have found that ANY one of the above reasons are enough to allow Fair Use. We have demonstrated that our use covers multiple rationales which courts have upheld as "strengthening the justification for an item's fair use."

As a side note, we were also told that our use herein would justify the reproduction of Joseph and Hyrum's exhumation photos and records (including their grisly remains) but as our intention is not to shock nor offend, we have chosen to continue to use William Whitaker's tracings instead.

The above rationale has been reviewed by attorney Paul Asay of Missouri.

Endnotes

[1] Of further interest on this point, I was once with an elder shaman of the Maori people of New Zealand. The *Book of Mormon* says that they are Lamanites. I asked the elder (shaman) to tell me the story of how his people came to the islands of Polynesia. He told me the story of the great ship builder who first brought the people west into the great sea. *Book of Mormon* readers will know his name as Hagoth. I then asked the shaman where the ship builder came from and he said, "From our homeland in the east. The great land of Uperu." He said that he was not sure where Uperu was but that it was a large continent far away to the east. It was not an island. I said could Uperu be *Peru*? That is east of New Zealand." He just stared at me for a while and then said, "I had never thought of that. You are very smart." Frederick G. Williams said that the Prophet Joseph told him that Lehi landed in the borders of what is today Chile and Elder Talmage said that Nephi's Land of First Inheritance was in what is today called Peru. I think the Maori Elders would now agree.

[2] Copyrights Book Entry #9810K, Library of Congress, Washington D.C. Note: Our ongoing research gives us reason to believe that Joseph Smith III used his father's daguerreotype to copyright the image of Joseph Smith the Prophet. The copyright laws of the time gave him this right as long as an image, including artwork, was sustained in its likeness to this daguerreotype.

[3] Naomi Rosenblum, A World History of Photography (New York: Abbeville Press, 1989) revised ed. 14-38. afterwards cited as Rosenblum also Helmut Gernsheim, Creative Photography Aesthetic Trends 1839-1960 (New York: Dover Publications, 1991) 32. afterwards cited as Gernsheim

[4] Rosenblum 47.

[5] Library of Congress, Special Collections.

[6] Reed Simonsen & Chad Fugate, Photograph Found A Concise History of the Joseph Smith Daguerreotype. (1993) 27. afterwards cited as Photograph Found

[7] David Haberstich Letter, Smithsonian Institute, August 17th 1993.

[8] Carma de Jong Anderson, personal interview, April 1994.

[9] Photograph Found "About the Cover."

[10] Haberstich Letter, August 17th 1993.

[11] Photograph Found 1-44.

[12] Gordon Baldwin, Looking At Photographs (J. Paul Getty Museum and British Museum Press, 1991) 35. also Naomi Rosenblum, A World History of Photography (New York: Abbeville Press, 1989) revised ed. 15. afterwards cited as Rosenblum.

[13] Richard N. Holzapfel & Jeffery Cottle, Old Mormon Nauvoo and Southern Iowa (Fieldbrook, 1991) 13.

[14] Joseph Smith Jr., History of the Church 2nd ed., vol. 4 (Salt Lake City, Deseret Book, 1980) 344. afterwards cited as: HC. HC 6:388-389.

[15] Joseph Smith III, letter to Joseph F. Smith, 26 October 1888. LDS Church History Department Archives.

[16] The Nauvoo Neighbor August 14th, 1844.

[17] Salt Lake Tribune 20 March 1910. also Joseph Smith III, letter to Joseph F. Smith, 26 October 1888. LDS Church History Department Archives.

[18] Ibid.

[19] Photograph Found 22-25.

[20] Rosenblum 38-53. and Helmut Gernsheim, Creative Photography Aesthetic Trends 1839-1960 (New York: Dover Publications, 1991) 28. afterwards cited as Gernsheim.

[21] Photograph Found (v. 1.3) 1-63.

[22] 21 Luke S. Johnson, "History of Luke Johnson by Himself." LDS Church Archives CR100-93-BX.2

[23] John Q. Cannon, George Cannon the Immigrant (Salt Lake City, 1927) 131. also Ephraim Hatch, "What did Joseph Smith Look Like?" Ensign March 1981: 65-73. afterwards cited as Ensign.

[24] Ensign 65-73.

[25] Personal interviews with Dr. Brent Lee DDS-Facial Surgeon, Dr. Steven Maloff MD:Plastic Surgeon, Dr. Charles Garrison M1):Forensic Pathologist and Richard Wheatley: Mortician.

[26] B. H. Roberts, A Comprehensive History of the Church 1930 ed., vol. 1 (SLC: Deseret Book, 1930) 281. afterwards cited as CHC. also George A. Smith, Journal of Discourses vol. 11 (Liverpool, 1867) 4-6. also History of Luke Johnson by Himself. LDS Church Archives CR100-93-BX.2 Mar 24th 1832.

[27] Photograph Found 1-45.

[28] Note: None of the official records or histories of the Church mention the Death Masks of the Martyrs being made. This has lead church scholars to question their authenticity, however, the similarities between the JS photograph and the Prophet's Death Mask serve to validate one another in numerous fascinating details.

[29] Dr. Brent Lee, Dr. Steven Maloff and Richard Wheatley; personal interview, 1993.

[30] Samuel O. Bennion, "To President Heber J. Grant," 21 Jan. 1928. also "Bodies of the Martyrs located." Saint's Herald 25 Jan 1928.

[31] Richard Howard, RLDS Historian, telephone conversation, Feb 1993.

[32] Special Thanks to Ronald E. Romig, RLDS Archivist.

[33] William Whitaker, letter to the authors, 13 Sept. 1993.

[34] HC 6:619-621.

[35] William M. Daniels, Correct Account of the Murders of Generals Joseph and Hyrum Smith at Carthage on the 27th Day of June 1844, (John Taylor: Nauvoo, 1845) 15.

[36] Lyman O. Littlefield, The Martyrs (SLC:1882) 87-90.

[37] Millennial Star 56:252-55.

[38] Dr. Charles Garrison M.D. Forensic Pathologist, personal interview, 1993.

[39] Andrew Jensen, Historical Record vol. 7:573-575.

[40] Salt Lake Tribune 20 March 1910.

[41] One critic pointed out that if Major had used photographs, and knew about the JS Photograph, why did he paint this particular Joseph Smith in profile? One can only speculate but it seems obvious that Major was intending to illustrate Joseph lecturing to the crowd. Portraying him frontally here would have defeated his purpose. Even so, Joseph in profile here is so reminiscent of Sutcliffe Maudsley's work that it begs the question, "Did Major borrow Maudsley in this instance?" The point is speculative but consistent with historical knowledge and illustrates our contention perfectly. See *Photograph Found: A Concise History of the Joseph Smith Daguerreotype* for more and detailed information.

[42] See *Lucy's Image: A Recently Discovered Photograph of Lucy Mack Smith* by Ronald E. Romig and Lachlan Mackay, *Journal of Mormon History V. 31, No. 27 (Fall 2005). pp. 61-77.* The authors met with Ron and Lach shortly after the discovery to discuss Joseph Smith. We found them to be both serious scholars and kind christians. They showed us these images and also said that they were re-examining an old photo in their archives called the Scannel Photo to see if it might be Joseph Smith. They asked us not to publish their discovery of Lucy until after they had had a chance to make an official study and public announcement. As excited as we were about Lucy, we wanted to respect their desire to "lead out" in this area. Despite the fact that their find greatly strengthened our case for the JS Photograph's authenticity, we agreed to keep quiet until they could prepare their announcement. Since the providence and historical facts surrounding Lucy's photo and painting are inartistically beneficial to our historical critique, and since the photo and painting have been publicly released since 2005, we feel it is appropriate to present them with our findings here. We also claim the right of Fair Use, for the reasons given herein as well.

[43] It is a Hollywood myth that subjects sat for weeks on end in front of a painter. The truth is that most painters would request a sitting and make numerous sketches. Then back at their studio, they would sketch in the major lines. After which, their apprentices would fill in the base and under painting. They would typically do the background, leaving the fine lines, skin tones and anything complicated for the master who would finish it and sign it. Not all artists worked this way. I had the pleasure of assisting modern master Arnold Friberg for a short time and he painted everything himself from man to native beadwork.

Made in the USA
San Bernardino, CA
24 July 2017